Restoring the Inner Heart

Restoring the Inner Heart

The Nous in Dostoevsky's Ridiculous Man

By
Mary Naumenko

HOLY TRINITY PUBLICATIONS
The Holy Trinity Seminary Press
Holy Trinity Monastery
Jordanville, New York
2019

Printed with the blessing of His Eminence,
Metropolitan Hilarion First Hierarch
of the Russian Orthodox Church Outside of Russia

Restoring the Inner Heart – The Nous in Dostoevsky's
Ridiculous Man © 2019 Mary Naumenko.

HOLY TRINITY
SEMINARY PRESS

An imprint of

HOLY TRINITY PUBLICATIONS
Holy Trinity Monastery
Jordanville, New York 13361-0036
www.holytrinitypublications.com

ISBN: 978-1-942699-12-5 (paperback)
ISBN: 978–1-942699–22-4 (ePub)
ISBN: 978–1-942699–23-1 (Mobipocket)

Library of Congress Control Number 2019938831

Cover Design: James Bozeman.
Cover Art: Integra Software Services Pvt. Ltd.

CONTENTS

INTRODUCTION

How human beings perceive spiritual phenomena has been the subject of study of poets, philosophers, and theologians throughout human history. Do we discern this with the mind, soul, heart, or an intuitive sixth sense? As far back as the pre-Socratic era (fifth and sixth centuries BC), this ability was often attributed to the *nous*. Later in history, we find the term *nous* in the epic poems of Homer, in Plato's dialogues, in Aristotle's writings, as well as in the works of the early fathers of the Christian Church.

The term *nous* is not easily defined for several reasons: it seeks to describe an inner function of human intuition for which many terms exist—mind, intellect, awareness, perception, reason, understanding. Its meaning has also evolved over time: it varied among early Greek philosophers and took on a different and deeper meaning within the understanding of the early Christian Church. It is a relatively obscure term today, used mostly by philosophers and theologians.

What is the *nous*, then? It is a God-given organ implanted deeply within each of us that is very receptive to the true reality of things. Within philosophy and metaphysics, the study of how things truly are is called *ontology*; *ontological* means relating to the true reality of what something is. Thus, one can also call the *nous* an "ontological receptor," because it is able to discern this reality to a greater or lesser degree. It is not only attuned to day-to-day reality but is especially adept at perceiving divine reality, that of the heavenly, spiritual realm. Ideally, its function is a form of insight or inner vision that instantly and correctly grasps the nature of a situation and its needs.[1] It follows, then, that the *nous* is a sensitive instrument of intuition that can bypass ordinary logical thinking and observation. Although considered by many to be centered within the human heart, it is greater than feelings or emotions: it is a higher form of cognition, a pure, intuitive grasp of that which is completely spiritual.

Why should we focus on the *nous*? The presence of the *nous* and its faculties gives rise to ultimate questions about human existence: Is there more to a human being than a body and soul? Can man directly experience the divine? A crucial question for us, living in the twenty-first century, is why the *nous*, the organ of discernment and spiritual vision within every person, so blatantly obvious to generations of philosophers and patristic writers of the Church is all but ignored today. With a closer look at the *nous*, the ontological receptor, our understanding of man and his spiritual potential can be deepened.

It was Anaxagoras of Clazomenae, born in Ionia about 500 BC, who gave the first clear, if limited, definition of *nous*. He was among the pre-Socratic Greek philosophers who explained the universe in terms of perpetual revolution of matter.[2] This philosopher postulated that all matter was mixed together in various concentrations throughout the universe and believed that *Nous* (intellect or mind) initiated its movement in the cosmos,[3] though he did not explain exactly how. Thus, Anaxagoras introduced an important principle into Greek philosophy: that of a universal power that directs all things. Over the following centuries, the understanding of the *nous* developed from this primitive conception to something higher and more subtle. In Hellenic philosophy, the *nous* was mostly considered a faculty of intuitive discernment.

The Incarnation of Jesus Christ, the Son of God, was the single event that wrought indelible changes in the history of mankind. Man now had much more direct access to God. It also deepened the understanding of the *nous*. According to the early Christian fathers, the corporeal heart is the center of a man's being, and it is the heart that contains the *nous*, the "eye of the soul."[4] The *nous* has also been termed "the spiritual mind or intuitive intellect,"[5] a "supra-rational capacity for knowing and experiencing, a spiritual intellect as distinct from the natural reason."[6] God's revelation comes primarily through this channel, and not through the limited human faculty of reason. In later Western Christian thought, it has been termed the *intellectus*.

During the last three hundred years, a more scholastic approach to religious and philosophic questions in our culture has frequently relied upon reason (*dianoia*) to come to knowledge of the truth.[7] Such a path, however, can be limited and deceptive. Certainly the discursive mind is involved, but it should be subservient to the heart. The twentieth-century Christian philosopher Ivan A. Ilyin[8] explains: "To have faith does not mean to reason about what one believes in, but to assuredly contemplate it within one's heart."[9] He also notes: "A holistic religious act cannot and should not exclude the mind. It cannot take place, however, if the mind does not learn to contemplate out of love."[10]

The current tendency is to learn *about* God, without realizing that one has the ability to experience His holiness in a much more direct way. According to the early Christian fathers, the *nous* is the organ present in all human beings, made specifically for such spiritual perception. It is defined, as said earlier, as the "eye of the soul," which in its purest state can directly reflect God's energy, a state of deification, also called *theosis* in Greek.[11] These same Church fathers often speak of the inconstancy of the natural reason (*dianoia*) and invoke the discernment of the *nous* to filter thoughts that either distract one or lead one away from God. This book focuses on the ontological receptor, the *nous*, in order to renew our trust in its intuitive powers, for its importance outweighs the logical reasoning that people have come to rely upon so much today.

There is one short story by the famous nineteenth-century novelist Fyodor Dostoevsky, which particularly exemplifies the power of *nous*. In "The Dream of a Ridiculous Man," the last and perhaps the most religious and profound of his short stories, Dostoevsky articulates a curious observation about the human perception of spiritual truth. (The entire text of this story in English translation appears in the appendix of this book.) It is a revelation to a man that happens apart from human reasoning and intellectual processing of information. The spiritual condition of the protagonist[12] is completely changed by a *dream*, following which he unabashedly asserts that he knows the truth. Prior to falling asleep he is a nihilistic[13] atheist about to commit suicide; following the dream he is a firm believer in God who wants to dedicate his life to sharing this truth with others. To be so utterly changed by the contents of a dream defies all logic. This cannot be a simple dream, but a vision of spiritual reality, an authentic, religious experience sent specifically to this individual in the *form* of a dream. It is the *nous*, or the eye of the soul, located in the heart, which is capable of apprehending revelation so directly. Although Dostoevsky does not use the term, it becomes apparent that in "The Dream" it is precisely the *nous*, as understood in the Eastern Orthodox tradition, which holds the key to the protagonist's transformation.

From Dostoevsky's biography, we learn to what a great extent his worldview was shaped by the Eastern Orthodox Church, whose beliefs follow the teachings of the early Christian fathers. In the patristic understanding, the *nous* is specifically "located within the bodily heart as in an organ."[14] Therefore, when these Holy Fathers discuss the *nous*, it is often interchangeable with the word *heart*. For example, in his Homily 17, St Gregory Palamas (1296–1359 AD) equates the two terms: "When we pay heed to the teaching of the Holy Spirit … we ponder them in our *nous*, which is to say our heart."[15] Similarly, in Step Six of *The Ladder*, the spiritual classic about asceticism, St John Climacus (579–649 AD) writes: "To have an insensitive heart is to have dulled the *nous*."[16]

It should not surprise us that Dostoevsky does not mention the word *nous* directly. It is a theological term that is not commonly used within the Orthodox Christian tradition and is preserved only in Greek liturgical books. By focusing so intently on the inner state of the heart of the protagonists within his literary works, Dostoevsky shows his compliance with the patristic teaching on the significance of the human heart, which can also be termed the *nous*. It is this patristic definition, shared by Dostoevsky, that is primarily examined in this book.

Because the concept of *nous* is illustrated here through Dostoevsky's literary description of a dream, a note of caution is in order. In the Eastern patristic tradition a belief in dreams is generally discouraged, lest it makes one prey to demonic deception. St Ignatius Brianchaninov (1807–1867) writes: "He who believes in dreams is completely inexperienced. But he who distrusts all dreams is a wise man. Only believe dreams that warn you of torments and judgment. But if despair afflicts you, then such dreams are also from demons."[17] On the other hand, the same author notes: "Dreams sent by God bring with them an irrefutable conviction or certainty."[18] It is the latter type of dream that Dostoevsky describes in "The Dream of a Ridiculous Man."

The use of dreams is not a new phenomenon in literature. It is found in Greek mythology,[19] in Holy Scripture,[20] as well as in contemporary prose. Dreams in both fiction and nonfiction can be used to impart a message of metaphysical significance to an individual. One familiar example is Charles Dickens's *A Christmas Carol.*[21] It is through nocturnal visions of ghosts that Ebenezer Scrooge comes to mend his covetous ways. Naturally, the author of fiction is at liberty to use dreams as he sees fit within the text: for example, in *The Iliad*, Book Two, a dream sent by Zeus to Agamemnon is not a revelation, but the god's trick to deceive him.[22]

Mortimer Adler, in *The Syntopicon of the Great Books of the Western World*, says the following regarding dreams:

> The nature and causes of dreaming are perennial themes in the tradition of western thought. As different suppositions are made concerning the cause of dreams, so different interpretations are given of their content. When it is supposed that the dream is inspired by gods or is a divine visitation, it becomes a medium of divination or prophecy, a way of foretelling the future, or of knowing what the gods intend in general, *or for the guidance of some particular man* [emphasis added]. In the great books of ancient poetry and history, and in the Old Testament as well, dreams, like oracles, are interpreted as supernatural portents, and figure as one of the major sources of prophecy.[23]

This quote strongly suggests that certain dreams were interpreted as divine revelation only in antiquity, in the tales of Greek mythology, or in Holy Scripture. Yet Dostoevsky's story is not one of distant past history or biblical times. The fact that a revelation can be imparted through a dream is a very significant aspect of this story. It can happen apart from any deductive reasoning, and it occurs through the discernment of the heart. By using a dream to impart wisdom to the protagonist, the author is suggesting that such revelation to the *nous* is still possible for contemporary man.

Although Dostoevsky's "The Dream of a Ridiculous Man" is a work of fiction, the author is clearly attempting to impart a spiritual lesson to his readers. Written in 1877, at the end of the novelist's literary career, this story may be considered a summation of the spiritual insight that he had acquired over the course of his life. According to Dostoevsky's biographer Joseph Frank: "'The Dream of a Ridiculous Man' contains Dostoevsky's most vibrant and touching depiction of his positive moral-religious ideal, expressed far more convincingly in this rhapsodic and 'fantastic' form than anywhere else in his work."[24]

Part I of this book presents a brief historical background of the concept of *nous*: how it changed as it moved through the channels of Hellenic philosophical thought and eventually transformed itself into a Christian concept of the "eye of the soul" as defined by the early Fathers of the Church. The reasons why *nous* has become a relatively obscure term in our Western culture are likewise considered. Part II begins with some relevant details of Dostoevsky's biography, followed by a synopsis of his short story. It is analyzed from the perspective of the existence of the *nous* as an organ of spiritual discernment within the human heart. The literary analysis then extends to further examples of "ridiculous" characters that appear in Dostoevsky's larger novels, those who also experience sudden revelations to the *nous*: Prince Myshkin of *The Idiot*, Alyosha in *The Brothers Karamazov*, and the formidable Stavrogin in *Demons*. Part III gives three examples of the unnamed *nous* in the more contemporary writings of Josef Pieper, William F. Lynch, and C.S. Lewis. It briefly discusses current renewed interest in deification among Western Christian denominations and concludes with some thoughts by present-day Orthodox authors on the subject of *nous*.

There has been a revival of this concept within the Eastern Orthodox tradition. This term comes up more and more frequently in contemporary writings on spiritual life. It presents a more complete vision of man and his spiritual potential. Let us take a closer look at the *nous* as viewed by early philosophers, Church Fathers, and author Fyodor Dostoevsky.

PART I

The History of the Concept of *Nous*
from Pre-Socratic Philosophy
to the Christian Era

CHAPTER 1

The *Nous* in Hellenic Philosophy: Anaxagoras to Plato

When portraying a direct spiritual revelation to the heart, Dostoevsky is not presenting anything new. In fact, the concept of *nous* has been with us for at least 2,500 years. It has been defined by philosophers both as the source of ontological truth and as an individual soul's receptor of the truth. Some use it interchangeably according to context. Thus, the *nous* was initially closely tied to the philosopher's explanation of the universe, an intrinsic subject of study for every philosophical school. Subsequently, the concept of *nous* survived the transition from philosophic religious thought to the Christian era, becoming central to the understanding of spiritual perception among the early Church Fathers. It is still evident in the Eastern Orthodox Christian tradition today. Fyodor Dostoevsky's religious views were firmly grounded within this tradition. By tracing the path of *nous* from its philosophic beginnings to its religious significance within Eastern Orthodoxy, this book seeks to provide a context for a deeper understanding of Dostoevsky's message in "The Dream of a Ridiculous Man."

One comes across the term *nous* frequently in the early Greek poetry of Homer (c. 750 BC), Aeschylus (525–456 BC), and Sophocles (496–406 BC). In Homeric poems alone it appears over one hundred times.[25] In *The Iliad*, for example, when speaking of the Muses, Polydamas tells Hector: "To one man the god has given works of war ... but in the heart of another, far-seeing Zeus has placed an excellent noos [*sic*]."[26] We see that even Homer located the *nous* within the heart! When discussing Homer's view of man, Homeric scholar Bruno Snell says the following concerning the *nous*:

> *Noos* [*sic*] is akin to *noein*, which means "to realize," to see in its true colors and often may simply be translated as "to see." It stands for a type of seeing which involves not only merely visual activity, but the mental act which goes with vision ... . Hence, the significance of noos. It is the mind as a recipient of clear images, or more briefly, the organ of clear images.[27]

In Greek tragedies, the *nous* is said to be present in gods and human beings. Its chief activity is intellectual and intuitive. "It can penetrate appearances to see what remains hidden to the eye."[28]

Pre-Socratic Greek philosophers also mention the *nous* in their writings. Heraclitus (c. fifth century BC) complained that "much learning does not teach *nous*."[29] Parmenides (early to mid-fifth century BC) used vocabulary related to the *nous*: the verb *noein*, as well as related words such as *noema* (thought) and *noetos* (thinkable). He distinguishes between opinion based on sense perception (*doxa*) and truth (*aletheia*). Noetic thinking is connected to "true discourse, valid reasoning and the cognition of reality."[30] It is apparent that these early thinkers associated the *nous* with deep knowledge of the true reality of things.

As mentioned in the Introduction, Anaxagoras of Clazomenae was the first pre-Socratic philosopher to speak of the *nous* in a definitive way. "Nous or Mind has power over all things that have life, both greater and smaller. And Nous had power over the whole revolution, so that it began to revolve at the start."[31] Anaxagoras also says: "Nous is infinite and self-ruled, and is mixed with nothing, but is alone, itself by itself ... the finest of all things and the purest, and it has all knowledge about everything and the greatest power."[32] However, Anaxagoras "never rose above the conception of a corporeal principle. He made Nous purer than other material things, but never reached the idea of an immaterial or incorporeal thing."[33] Other scholars dispute this on the grounds that Anaxagoras may simply not have made a sharp distinction between mind and matter.[34] Although he did not develop this principle fully, the introduction of Anaxagoras's *Nous* may have laid the foundation of later philosophical theism.[35]

Already in Plato (c. 428–c. 348 BC), the term *nous* is used both in the sense of an organizing force in the cosmos and as the highest part of a human soul. In Plato's *Phaedo*, his teacher Socrates favors the idea that "*nous* has organized the universe in the best possible way."[36] In Plato's main theological work *Timaeus, nous* plays a key role. As he regards the beauty and order in the universe, Plato attributes it to "the handiwork of a Divine Craftsman, *dêmiourgos*."[37] The results of this creation are so excellent that Plato is convinced that it is "the outcome of the deliberate intent of Intellect (*nous*)."[38] Thus, the *nous* is among his terms for God, interchangeable with *dêmiourgos*, Intellect or Divine Craftsman. Here Plato foreshadows the Christian understanding of God the Creator and the beauty of His creation.

In *Phaedrus*, Plato presents a metaphor for the human soul: a charioteer with a white horse on the right and a black horse on the left.[39] This illustrates the three parts or functions of the soul as envisioned by Plato: the rational, courageous or spirited, and appetitive.[40] The charioteer represents the *nous*, the rational, ruling force.[41] The high-spirited noble white horse is the part of the soul associated with challenges, courage, and honor; the ugly black horse represents all manner of appetites and pleasures. Some parallels in the future Christian understanding of the soul are reflected here as well: the *nous* is placed above and in control of various passions.

Plato's metaphysical reality envisions Forms or Ideas, universals that are higher and more real than what we see in the physical world around us. Our earthly vision sees but images of these Forms or Archetypes. For Plato, it is the *nous* that is capable of perceiving this higher metaphysical truth. The Analogy of the Divided Line, described in Book VI of Plato's *Republic*, illustrates the different levels of cognition in Plato's understanding:

PLATO'S ANALOGY OF THE DIVIDED LINE

	Objects	Mental States
Intelligible World	The Good	Intelligence (*noēsis*) or Knowledge (*epistēmē*)
	Forms	
	Mathematical Objects	Thinking (*dianoia*)
World of Appearances	Visible Things	Belief (*pistis*)
	Images	Imagining (*eikasia*)

Source: Plato, *Republic*, Book VI, The University of Adelaide Library.[42]

We see that the Intelligible World and the World of Appearances are divided by a horizontal line. Note that the bisection is not equal: Plato makes the Intelligible World larger and places it above the World of Appearances, thereby stressing its importance. What we observe and imagine is in our physical World of Appearances, on the lower, smaller plane. These observations are mere shadows of what lies above. Within the Intelligible World Plato places metaphysical phenomena (The Good, the Forms) and Mathematics, attributing its understanding to a more abstract form of thinking (*dianoia*). The apprehension of Forms and The Good he attributes to an even higher form of contemplation, *noēsis or epistēmē*.

Here is how one author interprets the Divided Line Analogy:

What Plato seems to be saying in the Divided Line is that there is a special form of knowledge, *noesis*, which is a much better basis for guiding our thoughts and actions than other, lesser forms of knowledge. What is far more subtle and interesting, and what is therefore perhaps more important for Plato here, is the contrast between *dianoia*, ordinary discursive ratiocination, and *noesis*.

This distinction is vital. While *dianoia* thinking certainly has benefits, we have a distinct tendency to over-rely on it and to forget its limitations. The weakness of *dianoia* is that it must begin by taking as true unproven assumptions. We are, in effect, presupposing a model of reality before we begin our deliberations. But any model, be it logical, geometrical, or moral, is only imperfect. Its conclusions may be, and frequently are, wrong … . In contrast, *noesis* presupposes a soul that has turned away from specific selfish concerns to seek the Good itself.[43]

In Book VII of his *Republic*, Plato presents another metaphor for the cognitive perception of truth: the allegory of the cave. Human beings are shown as prisoners in a dark cave, chained to a wall so that they cannot turn around. The only light which enters the cave is from a fire at the cave's entrance far above. Because of this light source the prisoners perceive shadows as real persons and things. One of them is freed to leave the cave and comes out into the brilliant light of truth. When he comes back to tell the other prisoners of the full reality of things, they resist the truth, laugh at him, tell him he has become corrupted, and even threaten to kill him.[44] He has become a ridiculous man. We shall see a reflection of this metaphor in Dostoevsky's short story.

Philip Sherrard gives us further insight on Plato's vision of the world:

> The Platonic universe is really a hierarchy of Images, all co-existing, each issuing from and sharing in the one above it, from the highest supra-essential realities down to those of the visible world. It is this structure of participation which constitutes the great golden chain of being, that unbroken connection between the highest and the lowest heaven and earth. In this structure there is nothing that is not animate, nothing that is mere dead matter. All is endowed with being, all—even the last particle—belongs to a living and transmuting whole.[45]

Sherrard goes on to explain that upon this basis, the interconnectedness of the highest with the lowest within the Platonic universe that the early Christian Fathers were better able to conceptualize man as created in the image of God, as well as our Lord Jesus Christ being of two natures, fully God and fully man. "It was against this background of Platonic understanding about how the image participates in the archetype that the conception of man as created in the image of God received a new and more positive content in the Christian idea of God-manhood."[46]

We witness a great development of philosophical thought on the *nous* from Anaxagoras to Plato. For Anaxagoras, *Nous* was a vague form of power that moved the universe. For Plato, *nous* is both a name for the Divine Craftsman and the highest part of the human soul in charge of all its other faculties. It also becomes apparent how certain future aspects of Christian teaching were rooted in a Platonic understanding of the universe.

CHAPTER 2

The *Nous* in Hellenic Philosophy: Aristotle to Plotinus

Much like his predecessors, the philosopher Aristotle (384–322 BC) defines *nous* both as a cosmic ruling force and as part of the human soul. Anaxagoras's *Nous* as the ambiguous Good Principle that moves the cosmos is refined by Aristotle. He postulates what he calls the First Unmoved Mover. He has much to say concerning the characteristics of this Prime Mover in both his works *Physics* and *Metaphysics*.

By definition, the First *Unmoved* Mover is not set in motion by any other entity. Because Aristotle believed motion to be everlasting, so the Unmoved Mover must also be eternal.[47] Through constantly fulfilling its potential of creating movement in the universe, Aristotle implies that "the Unmoved Mover is constituted by eternal love, wisdom and fulfillment."[48] He attributes to it the highest forms of thinking.[49] For all these reasons, it is evident why Aristotle refers to this Prime Mover as God.

With respect to human beings, Aristotle describes the *nous* as "the part of the soul by which it knows and understands."[50] In conjunction with this he proposes two different modes of human reasoning, passive and active.[51] The passive intellect is associated with everyday thinking and sense perception: it involves both the soul and body. By contrast, the *nous* is active and creative, and "can grasp pure forms immediately and without the aid of imagery."[52] Once again one is reminded of the intuitive capacities of the *nous*, as noted in the earlier quotes from Homer. According to Aristotle, this active form of intellect, the *nous*, can exist outside of the body. It alone is divine.[53] Scholars still debate what Aristotle meant the active intellect to be: "an aspect of the human soul or an entity existing independently of man."[54]

Aristotle attributes the grasp of the basic premises of analytical science to the *nous*.[55] But by far the loftiest use of the *nous* for Aristotle is divine contemplation, *theoria*, for this promotes the greatest happiness (*eudaimonia*). Aristotle considered any man who neglected to engage in *theoria* to be seriously impoverished as a human being:

> Such a life would be beyond a man. For it is not as being a man that he will live in that way, but in so far as something divine is present in him; and as this divine element (*nous*) is superior to our composite human nature, so its activity (*theoria*) is superior to activity displaying the other sort of excellence (good action). If reason is divine, then, in comparison with man, the life of reason is divine in comparison with human life.
>
> Yet we must not—as some advise—think just of human things because we are human, and of mortal things because we are mortal. Rather we must, as far as we can, make ourselves immortal, and we must do everything possible to live in accordance with the best thing in us (*nous*). For however small in bulk it may be, in power and value it surpasses everything.[56]

For Aristotle, the *nous* is strongly associated with the divine. It is both a Prime Mover in the universe and the organ of loftiest thought in human beings, capable of reaching the greatest fulfillment.

However, Aristotle's whole approach to philosophy was logical and categorical. This significantly affected how the *nous* was understood by future philosophers and theologians in the West. The operations of reason began to dominate. The basis of this shift in thinking was Aristotle's teaching on form, substance, and matter. It was a departure from the Platonic understanding of the material and spiritual world. Recall that Plato envisioned a world of a "hierarchical system of forms,"[57] from the highest intelligible Ideas to the smallest particle, all as part of an integrated chain of being. Aristotle rejected Plato's Forms, the possibility of a relationship of an image (in the visible world) with its ideal archetype (in the heavenly realm). "For Aristotle, forms do not exist independently of things … A 'substantial' form is a kind that is attributed to a thing, without which that thing would be of a different kind or would cease to exist altogether."[58]

According to Philip Sherrard, in contrast to Plato's Universals of the Intelligible World, the Aristotelian view of universals is simply a category, "an abstract class name … no universals exist apart from concrete particulars and no universal is a substance. It is impossible for a universal to be a substance because, according to Aristotle, the substance of a thing is peculiar to that thing, whereas the Platonic universal is by definition that which can be present in a multiplicity of things."[59] Sherrard sees the Platonic worldview as instrumental in formulating the Christian doctrine on the Incarnation of the Son of God and deification of man. It is his conviction that the application of

Aristotelian principles to Christian teaching, as happened in the West beginning in the twelfth century, drastically altered the understanding of the faith as originally set forth in the early patristic writings.[60] It also changed the perception of the capabilities of the *nous* within the human heart. We shall come back to this consideration in Chapter 7.

Next we move our focus to Alexandria, to a time that roughly corresponds with the coming of Jesus of Nazareth into the world. It was this great cosmopolitan city in Egypt that became the center of Jewish-Hellenic philosophy, the Neoplatonism of Plotinus,[61] and subsequently gave rise to the first Christian philosophers.

In Alexandria, the process of reconciliation of Greek philosophy and the Jewish Scriptures began. Its chief philosopher was Philo of Alexandria (25 BC–40 AD), who taught that God is personal, but Pure Being at the same time.[62] Philo's idea of the *nous* was tied in with the Logos, God's instrument for the formation of the world.[63] The Platonic Ideas are also placed in the *nous*, or Logos.[64] Philo insisted that Greek philosophy had borrowed much from Holy Scripture and claimed the knowledge as its own.[65] Although Philo's idea of Logos was still far from the Christian conception, his teaching emphasizes some aspects that were accepted by Christianity:

> Philo … insists on the necessity of man's liberating himself from the power of the sensual … . [H]e emphasized trust in God rather than trust in oneself. Virtue then is to be pursued and man's task is to attain the greatest possible likeness to God. … [A]bove conceptual knowledge of God is to be ranked heavenly wisdom or the immediate intuition of the ineffable Godhead. This is an interior task …

The passive state of ecstasy thus becomes the highest stage of the soul's life on earth, as it was later to be in the Neoplatonic philosophy.[66]

Philo's teaching prepared the way for the Neoplatonist school of philosophical thought, whose founder was Plotinus.[67] According to this philosophy, God is absolutely transcendent, the One, beyond all thought and all being, ineffable and incomprehensible.[68] The first emanation from the One is Thought or Mind, *Nous*, which is intuition or immediate apprehension.[69] *Nous* is identified with the Demiurge of Plato's *Timaeus*, and the whole multitude of Ideas is found in the *nous*. Plotinus also incorporates Aristotelian concepts. Thus, he divides the human soul into three elements—body, soul, and spirit—the highest of which belongs to the sphere of the *nous*. Because the soul enters into direct union with the body, it is contaminated by matter and requires ethical ascent. By following the four cardinal virtues,[70] a soul frees itself of carnality and takes its flight to a mystical ecstatic union with God.[71] In Plotinus one finds "a syncretism of Plato's forms with Aristotle's Unmoved Mover."[72]

Neoplatonism, though a competing school of thought with Christianity, takes a significant step toward it. For Plotinus, "mystical experience is the supreme attainment of the true philosopher, philosophy tends to pass into religion: at least it points beyond itself: '*speculation does not set itself up as the ultimate goal to be achieved* [italics added].'"[73]

A good illustration appears in Plotinus's *First Ennead:*

He that has the strength, let him arise and withdraw into himself, foregoing all that is known by the eyes, turning away from the material beauty that once made his joy ... The Fatherland to us is There whence we have come, and

There is The Father. What then is our course, what the manner of our flight? This is not a journey for the feet; the feet bring us only from land to land; ... the Soul must be trained—to the habit of remarking, first, all noble pursuits, then the works of beauty produced not by the labor of the arts but by virtue of men known for their goodness. Lastly, you must search the souls of those that have shaped these beautiful forms.[74]

Plotinus compares the formation of a beautiful soul with the chiseling of a statue:

The sculptor cuts away here, he smoothes there, he makes this line lighter, this other purer, until a lovely face has grown upon his work. So do you also: cut away all that is excessive, straighten all that is crooked, bring light to all that is overcast, labor to make all one glow of beauty and never cease chiseling your statue, until there shall shine out of you from it the godlike splendor of virtue, until you shall see the perfect goodness surely established in the stainless shrine.[75]

Here is an evident prefiguration of the Christian patristic understanding of the soul (or the *nous*) encountering God. There is, however, one key element for a Christian that is missing in Plotinus: withdrawing into ourselves (achieving inner stillness, *hesychia*, as the Fathers of the Church later defined it) must be accompanied by prayer to our Saviour; and chiseling ourselves into virtuous human beings can only be accomplished with the help of our Lord Jesus Christ, in whom all virtue was manifested to the greatest possible degree. Without this focus on Jesus Christ, every human being inevitably falls into the sin of pride, attributing the skill of the chiseler to himself. Holy Scripture teaches that "God resists the proud, but gives grace to the humble" (James 4:6). Still, one must admire the insights of Plotinus, whose conceptions paved the way from Hellenic to Christian philosophy.

CHAPTER 3

A Transition from Hellenic Philosophy to Christianity

Enlightened thinkers of the first centuries of our era faced the challenge of reconciling their philosophical under-standing of wisdom with the newly emergent Christian faith. The second-century Christian apologist Justin Martyr was pro-foundly moved (and converted to Christianity) by the behavior of Christians, "for they exhibited a superiority to revenge and hate entirely unaccountable, praying for their enemies, seeking to glorify their God by love to their fellow men."[76] His position was that pagan philosophy, especially Platonism, is not alto-gether wrong, but is a partial grasp of the truth and serves as "a schoolmaster to bring us to Christ."[77]

Other philosophers were converted in the process of trying to refute Christianity. Such was the case of Athenagoras the Great of Alexandria (133–190 AD). Philip of Side (380–431 AD), an historian of the early Christian Church, writes about him: "This man … was eager to write against the Christians, but when he read the divine Scriptures in order to make his arguments more precisely, he was seized by the Holy Spirit in such a way that, like the great Paul, he became a teacher instead of a persecutor of the faith which he was persecuting."[78] Athenagoras converted to Christianity and became the first dean of the Christian Theological School in Alexandria.

Another great teacher and thinker of the same institution was Saint Clement of Alexandria (150–215 AD), who staunchly defended the study of pagan philosophy but in light of Christian teachings. Clement describes philosophy as a "co-operator" in the search for truth:

> As many men drawing down the ship, cannot be called many causes, but one cause consisting of many;—for each individual by himself is not the cause of the ship being drawn, but along with the rest;—so also philosophy, being the search for truth, contributes to the comprehension of truth; not as being the cause of comprehension, but a cause along with other things, and co-operator; perhaps also a joint cause.[79]

Many Christian apologists, following the example of the Alexandrian school, applied what was valuable in Greek philosophy to give Christian thought a more definitive expression. The influence of Plato and Aristotle is evident throughout these writings, for they exhibit a philosophical literary style or a form of argumentation favored by these eminent Hellenic philosophers.[80] However, they do this with discernment. St Basil the Great says that just as bees gather honey from some flowers and pass over others, so should we, "having appropriated from (pagan) literature what is suitable for us and akin to the truth, pass over the remainder."[81]

There were obvious contradictions between Hellenic and Christian teaching, which Apostle Paul so adamantly sets forth in 1 Corinthians: "I will destroy the wisdom of the wise, and bring to nothing the understanding of the prudent … Greeks seek after wisdom; but we preach Christ crucified..." (1 Cor 1:19–23). As theologian Vladimir Lossky states, "Revelation sets an abyss between the truth it declares and the truths which can be discovered by philosophical speculation."[82] For the Greek philosophers, wisdom resided in the realm of intelligibles[83] or solely with the gods/divinities. By contrast, the Christian era ushers forth a new and profound understanding of the Holy Trinity. The Lord Jesus Christ, Who Himself is Wisdom Incarnate, appears on earth. He teaches people about God the Father and the Holy Spirit. He overcomes the power of death by His own death on the Cross. He rises from the dead and reopens for man the gates of paradise, restoring in him "the image that fell of old."[84] "The new essence which Christ reveals in man opens the way for the mystical journey of the Christian. His (man's) struggle and his aim are to become as much as possible a better and more complete imitator of His Lord and Saviour, Jesus Christ."[85]

CHAPTER 4

The Incarnation and Deification
in Early Patristic Thought

The Incarnation of our Lord Jesus Christ, the Son of God, lays the cornerstone for the building of the Christian tradition. There is a profound change in man's capacity to relate to God, and the *nous* as "the eye of the soul"[86] and organ of spiritual discernment within every human being remains central in this discussion.

St Irenaeus of Lyons (130–202 AD) is one of the first to express the great significance of this event for man. He exhorts us to follow "the only true and steadfast Teacher, the Word of God, our Lord Jesus Christ, who did, through His transcendent love, become what we are, that He might bring us to be even what He is Himself."[87] Some two hundred years later, St Athanasius of Alexandria (297–373 AD) echoes St Irenaeus in his treatise *On the Incarnation*: "The Word was made man that we might be made God."[88] St Symeon the New Theologian (949–1022 AD) explains this further in his Homily 45, "Adam and the First Created World":

> Inasmuch as our Lord Jesus Christ became perfect man in soul and body, like us in everything except sin, so He gives of His Divinity to us also who believe in Him, and makes us like unto Him in the nature and essence of His Divinity.

Reflect on this most wondrous mystery: the Son of God received from us flesh, which He did not have by nature, and became man, which He was not, and to those who believe in Him He communicates of His Divinity, which no man had in any way—and these believers are gods by grace. For Christ gives them *to be the sons of God*, as John the Theologian says. (John 1:12, I John 3:2)[89]

This is the basis of the patristic teaching on deification (also referred to as *theosis* or divinization), the transformative potential for human beings to unite with God and to reflect His divinity. Similar thoughts are found in the writings of St Clement of Alexandria, St Basil the Great, St Gregory of Nazianzus, and St Maximus the Confessor.[90] Philip Sherrard explains this in more contemporary form and thereby gives us a patristic Christian definition of man:

What Christ is by nature—this divine-human reality whose subject is the Logos of God—man is by filiation, by participation. This is the image, as it were, in which man is created. Man is a creature created to be the son of God. He is born to be free of the sphere of death and corruption. Death and corruption are profoundly alien to his nature; they are profoundly unnatural to him. What is natural to him is precisely that eternal life which is through participation in the divine. This deification of man is realized only in relationship to that unique divine-human reality who is Christ ... insofar as man fails to realize the divine in himself, to that extent he falls short of being completely human.[91]

Sherrard goes on to say that the very "idea that man can be human apart from God is a false idea ... The very concept of man implies a relationship, a connection with God."[92] Our Lord

Jesus Christ not only comes to save mankind from death and corruption; through taking on human form, He grants us the ability to share in His divinity. It is within this context that Sherrard introduces the ontological receptor, the *nous*, calling it the spiritual intellect:

> Patristic theologians ... affirm that he (man) possesses, whether he is aware of it or not, whether he develops it or not, a supra-rational capacity for knowing and experiencing, a spiritual intellect as distinct from the natural reason. This spiritual intellect is, they say, the God-like faculty in man, the spirit breathed into him by the Holy Spirit in the act of his creation and that which in the deepest part of himself he is. They describe this organ or faculty as dwelling in the depths of the soul, as the eye of the soul, and as constituting the innermost aspect of the heart, man's spiritual subject or "inner man" by means of which he is able to contemplate spiritual realities and even to attain direct union with God.[93]

In other words, man is not limited to know about God intellectually, but can directly experience the divine and can reflect God's energies through the purification of the *nous*. "The spiritual intellect knows all things through knowing their inner essences, through direct participation in the divine ideas or divine energies that bring them into being ... an immediate intuition and experience of the inner, eternal and absolute nature of everything that is."[94] This is not knowledge attainable by reason, as St Maximus the Confessor (580–662 AD) explains:

> The scriptural Word knows of two kinds of knowledge of divine things. On the one hand, there is relative knowledge, rooted only in reason and ideas, and lacking in the

kind of experiential perception of what one knows in active engagement; such relative knowledge is what we use to order our affairs in our present life. On the other hand there is that truly authentic knowledge, gained only by actual experience, apart from reason and ideas, which provides a total perception of the known object through a participation by grace.[95]

St Gregory Palamas writes extensively on *theosis*, confirming and further elucidating the thoughts of St Irenaeus, St Maximus, and other early Christian Fathers. The concept of *nous* plays a central role in his writings, for its purification is what renders such deification possible. St Gregory insists upon the capacity of the *nous* to be renewed and deified by the uncreated light of God. He maintains that God in His essence is unknowable by man, but man is able to partake of God's energies.[96] This energy is the grace of God, which is not "just a gift of God … but a direct manifestation of the living God Himself."[97] Professor David Bradshaw explains:

> One of the most notable features of Eastern Orthodox theology is the distinction drawn by St. Gregory Palamas between the divine essence (οὐσία) and energies (ἐνέργειαι). The divine essence is God as He is in Himself, unknowable not only to man but to any created intellect; the energies are God as He manifests Himself and gives Himself to be shared by creatures.[98]

It is this specific patristic teaching on *theosis*, the potential for human deification, that fired Dostoevsky's soul and imagination. As we shall see in "The Dream of a Ridiculous Man," divine revelation works a complete change of heart (*nous*) in the protagonist.

CHAPTER 5

The Heart and the *Nous* in Patristic Thought

Although Greek philosophers acknowledged the *nous* to be the faculty of the apprehension of God, it was never consistently associated with the heart.[99] It is in the Bible that the heart plays "a rich and multifaceted role, and most patristic Fathers follow its lead."[100] The Holy Fathers emphasize the heart, in the sense that it includes man's entire being—not only intellect but will, emotions, and even the body.[101] It is therefore not surprising that St Macarius of Egypt (301–391 AD) locates the *nous* within the heart:

> Whenever grace fully possesses the pastures of the heart, it rules over all the members and thoughts; for there, in the heart, the intellect (*nous*) abides as well as all the thoughts of the soul and all its hopes, and from the heart grace penetrates throughout all the parts of the body.[102]

One thousand years later, St Gregory Palamas writes: "The heart of man is the controlling organ, the throne of grace. The *nous* and all the thoughts of the soul are to be found there."[103] Note how this teaching of the Fathers remains consistent over the centuries. It is from this perspective that Dostoevsky discusses the heart in his short story, the heart that contains the *nous*.

27

One may wonder, if in patristic thought the heart is so central to man's entire being, how is it to be differentiated from the mind? Discursive reasoning is the more accepted instrument for perceiving truth within contemporary Western culture. Professor David Bradshaw explains: "The fact that the heart is a physical organ which we do not see, but whose power wells up from within, not only makes it deep and hard to know; it also makes it capable of receiving mysteries in a way that the conscious mind is not."[104] He unravels the subtle distinctions between mind, *nous*, and heart within the New Testament Scripture:

> The Greek term *nous*, [is] the most common term for mind in the New Testament, and one that is central to the later Greek tradition. It bears a range of meanings: mind, reason, understanding, thought, judgment resolve and disposition. The best way to get a handle on its variety is to think of its meaning as related in various ways to the act of understanding. Specifically, it ranges from a) the *faculty* of understanding, to b) the *characteristic way* that faculty is exercised, to c) a *particular act* of its exercise, to d) the *virtue* of exercising it well. For example, when St. Paul quotes from the Greek translation of the prophet Isaiah "Who has known the mind (*nous*) of the Lord?" (1 Cor 2:16), he would seem to be referring to (c), the specific content of the divine mind. When he then goes on to declare triumphantly, "But we have the mind (*nous*) of Christ," he probably refers instead to (b), a characteristic way of thinking.[105]

Bradshaw goes on to explain that "because of its range of meanings, *nous* does not stand in opposition to feeling or emotion in the same way as does 'mind' in English."[106] In particular, he points to a citation in Romans 7:23, where Apostle Paul speaks of the "law of my mind (*nous*)" that opposes the law of sin in his members. *Nous* in this sense is a "faculty of understanding specifically insofar as it is correct and true ... it seems to echo the usage of *nous* among philosophical authors, for whom *nous* is a faculty specifically fitted for communion with God."[107] According to Bradshaw, it is this meaning of *nous* that bridges the biblical and philosophical meanings of the term.

CHAPTER 6

Purification of the *Nous*

The mere existence of the *nous* within every human heart does not guarantee its proper function. It can be fully enlightened and active or completely darkened and dormant, depending on the state of its purity. It follows, then, that its condition will vary within each person in various stages of life. A young child's *nous* is likely more pure and sensitive than that of an adult. Perhaps this is one reason Jesus Christ sets a child in front of His disciples and says: "Assuredly, I say to you, unless you are converted and become as little children, you will by no means enter the kingdom of heaven" (Matthew 18:3).

How does one achieve the purification of the *nous*? This is a lifelong process and struggle for a believer in Christ. Clearly, the grace of God that the Church bestows through the mysteries of Holy Baptism and Chrismation is a crucial step, according to the Holy Fathers. St Symeon the New Theologian writes: "Thus each one who is baptized [once] again becomes such as Adam was before the transgression, and is led into the *noetic* [emphasis added] Paradise and receives the commandment to work it and keep it—to work it by the fulfillment of the commandments of Jesus Christ."[108]

Continuous effort is required to retain this baptismal paradisiacal state. Christians in all walks of life are called to the purification of the *nous* through the classic Christian disciplines of fasting, prayer, and almsgiving. However, few achieve the level of sanctity and purity to experience *theosis*. The *nous* is the organ that perceives God's grace, and the potential for sainthood is God-given, but is manifested in those who fully dedicate their hearts to love of God and neighbor. This naturally comes more easily to those who embrace monasticism, "whose aim is union with God in a complete renunciation of the life of this present world."[109]

Hesychasm, the practice of inner stillness, is what Christians have employed for centuries to increase the ability to concentrate on prayer. The Holy Fathers speak of the prayer of the heart, where the words are first only on the lips, but with increased effort of concentration on the meaning of the words, the prayer can descend into the heart (*nous*), where the intellect and heart become united.[110]

Through *hesychia* and constant concentrated inner prayer, the monastic saints are transformed or "deified" and partake of God's energies directly (*theosis*). The Divine light, which was made manifest for the apostles at the Transfiguration on Mount Tabor, can actually be seen by and emanate from one who has purified his *nous*. St Gregory Palamas explains:

> The human mind also ... transcends itself, and by victory over the passions acquires an angelic form. It, too will attain to that light and will become worthy of a supernatural vision of God, not seeing the divine essence, but seeing God by a revelation appropriate and analogous to Him.[111]

Saint Gregory confirmed this through his own direct experience by living as a strict ascetic and anchorite on the Holy Mountain of Athos. He was not formulating a new teaching but was elucidating and confirming the writings of the early Church Fathers.

St Maximus the Confessor writes: "The *nous* functions in accordance with nature when it keeps the passions under control, contemplates the inner essences of created beings, and abides with God."[112] In other words, one needs to exert all of one's energies and will in order, with God's help, to purify the *nous*. To be healed of the fallen state one must keep all of God's commandments. "Stillness, prayer, love and self-control are a four-horse chariot bearing the *nous* to heaven," says St Thalassios in the second book of his writings in the *Philokalia*.[113]

Herein is man's greatest challenge and difficulty: the *nous* was blackened, darkened, and sickened by the fall and lost this ability to function according to its nature. It has the freedom to choose between "virtue and vice, angel and demon."[114] In its fallen state, the *nous* is often blinded by the passions of avarice, self-esteem, and sensual pleasure.[115] It is made coarse by callousness, insensibility, and indifference and cannot pray to God purely. St Maximus the Confessor says that "just as a sparrow tied by the leg cannot fly, much as it tries, because it is pulled down to the ground, similarly, when the *nous* that has not yet attained dispassion flies up towards heavenly knowledge, it is held back by the passions and pulled down to earth."[116] If the *nous* is the eye of the soul, then just as bodily eyes need light to function, so too does the *nous* need the source of noetic light and Life, that is, the Lord Jesus Christ. In order to maintain the soul's purity, the *nous* must stand on guard at the entrance of the heart, ready to accept or reject extraneous thoughts provided by reason.

St Theophan the Recluse (1815–1894) explains this more thoroughly in his interpretation of a passage in Proverbs 6:5–6: "Do not give sleep to your eyes nor slumber to your eyelids that you may be saved, as a gazelle from the snares, and as a bird from the trap."

> Everyone who in his heart has set out now, before the face of the Lord, to live according to His commandments, should take this rule as a guide. He must not give sleep to his eyes—not these outer eyes, but the inner eyes of his mind—that they may gaze into his heart and faithfully observe all that occurs there, and thus he who is zealous will be able to find the enemy's snares and avoid danger from them. The heart now becomes an arena for struggle against the enemy. There the enemy unceasingly sows his own [seed], which is in turn reflected in one's thoughts.[117]

So the *nous* (referred to here as "the inner eyes of the mind") to the extent that it has been purified and has discernment is able to filter suggestions of the evil one as he attempts to pull one from one's resolve to serve God alone. His wiles are cunning and at times barely noticeable:

> Such thoughts, however, are not always outrageously bad, but are for the most part disguised by false goodness and correctness. The chain of all thoughts is like an intricate net! ... Take note of what your relentless "advisor" proposes to you on the left side and investigate the reason it was proposed to you and where it will lead, and you will never fall into his snares. Only, do not forget that attentiveness alone is not effective. It must be joined with abstinence, wakefulness and unceasing prayer to the Lord.

St Basil the Great (329–379 AD) writes in a letter to his friend, St Gregory of Nazianzus (330–389 AD): "The man whose *nous* is not dissipated upon extraneous things, not diffused over the world about us through the senses, withdraws within itself and of its own accord ascends to the contemplation of God."[118] This dissipated mind is rational and scattered thinking, which needs to be gathered together and returned to the *nous*. This becomes apparent to anyone who has attempted to pray with concentration. Thoughts scatter immediately and one becomes distracted. It takes much effort and the help of the grace of God to make the mind "effectually present to the heart, enabling the two to act as a unity in their natural and proper relationship."[119]

Why is this process so difficult? According to St Maximus, self-love is the mistress of all passions, which gives rise to three general passions: love of glory, avarice, and self-indulgence (the very same three temptations with which the devil approached Christ in the desert).[120] This is what interferes most with a firm connection to God. The goal is not to mortify the passions, or to deny that they exist, but to redirect them. Self-love must be transformed into love for God and neighbor. How difficult it is to stay focused on this active journey toward God in a world of constant flux and distractions. What a challenge this can be in an environment that idealizes material comfort and caters to all manner of self-indulgence!

CHAPTER 7

A Move Away from Noetic Perception

In modern translations of Greek playwrights and philosophers, *nous* is most often simply translated as *mind*. There is no distinction between the ontological and rational modes of knowledge. It is no wonder that hardly anyone today has heard of the term *nous*. It has literally been lost in translation. Lamentably, the use of the word *mind* instead of *nous* has erased the very concept of "a supra-rational capacity for knowing and experiencing, a spiritual intellect as distinct from the natural reason."[121] Even the ancient philosophers' understanding of *nous* as a faculty of intuitive discernment is obscured by the term *mind*, because most have come to associate the workings of the mind with mere logical thought.

From what time in history do we note a gradual waning of the significance of the *nous* and noetic perception? Philip Sherrard traces this departure back to the time of Blessed Augustine (354–430 AD), a revered saint in the Christian East and the most prominent Roman Catholic theologian of the West. Sherrard writes:

> It is one of the paradoxes, and also one of the tragedies of the western Christian tradition that the man who affirmed so strongly the presence of God in the depths of his own

self ... should as a dogmatic theologian have been responsible for "consecrating" within the Christian world the idea of man's slavery and impotence due to the radical perversion of human nature through original sin. It has been St. Augustine's theology which in the West has veiled down to the present day the full radiance of the Christian revelation of divine sonship—the full revelation who man essentially is.[122]

Because Blessed Augustine profoundly repented of his wayward life prior to his conversion (as he so eloquently relates in his *Confessions*), he was led to contrast man's baseness with God's holiness. He assumed a great separation between the human and the divine, precluding the possibility of divine sonship. His limited knowledge of the Greek language created an impediment to reading the works of the Eastern fathers, which led to some innovations in his own theology. One of these was his doctrine of divine simplicity,[123] which erased the patristic distinction between God's unknowable Essence and His divine energies.

Blessed Augustine was engaged in a long struggle against the heresy of Pelagius, "which denied the necessity of God's grace for salvation."[124] In reaction to Pelagius's error, Augustine overemphasized the role of God's grace. As Father Seraphim Rose († 1981) explains: "The fundamental error of Augustine was his *overstatement* of the place of grace in Christian life, and his *understatement* of the place of free will."[125] In other words, Blessed Augustine taught that salvation is more dependent upon God's actions than upon our own. By contrast, the Eastern Orthodox teaching on this is a synergistic "cooperation of Divine grace and human freedom, neither one acting independently or autonomously."[126] Synergy implies active participation on the part of both God and man. If, according to Augustine, God's Essence is unknowable and His energies cannot be directly experienced, how can man truly communicate with Him?

More relevant to our discussion on the *nous*, Augustine envisions within man a rational soul that is superior to the body but independent of it.[127] He attributes to this soul a faculty superior to reason, calling it the *intellectus*. However, this is not the *nous* as the Eastern fathers understood it.[128] "The deiform [divine] *nous*," writes Sherrard, "is heart centered and of an order essentially different from and superior to the psycho-physical whole of man, while the Augustinian intellect is but a superior mental faculty of the soul itself."[129] In Blessed Augustine's conception, the *intellectus* is capable of knowing God analogically as the cause of the natural, sensible world.[130] In other words, *intellectus* is a part of man's rational soul that can infer what God is like by observing His creation. This is closer to the philosophical, Aristotelian concept of *nous*.[131] The Greek patristic *nous*, on the other hand, acquires knowledge "which comprehends things in a truly universal sense ... by knowing their divine principles, not in an abstract or conceptual way, but by participation."[132]

Blessed Augustine's understanding of *intellectus* as a higher, intuitive aspect of the rational soul was shared by the Roman Catholic philosopher and theologian Thomas Aquinas (†1274), who remains an influential Roman Catholic saint and theologian to this day. He synthesized Aristotelian logic with the understanding of faith in his famous work *Summa Theologica*, where he carefully expounded upon Christian truths according to sound rules of philosophical argumentation.[133] His quest was to marry "faith and reason, revelation and philosophy, the Biblical and the classical inheritances."[134] Under the influence of Aquinas the emphasis began to shift away from the heart and intuition toward the logical operations of reason. "When he [Aquinas] speaks of speculative or theoretical knowledge, the emphasis seems to be far more on the discursive than on the intuitive."[135]

Thomas Aquinas equates reason and intellect in man, and attributes perfect knowledge of intelligible truth only to the angels:

> For to understand is simply to immediately apprehend intelligible truth; and to reason is to advance from one understood thing to another ... angels, who according to their nature possess perfect knowledge of intelligible truth have no need to advance from one thing to another, but apprehend the truth simply and without mental discussion ... but man arrives at the knowledge of intelligible truth by advancing from one thing to another; and therefore he is called rational.[136]

However, in both philosophic and patristic definitions of *nous*, man *is* capable of immediate apprehension of truth, akin to that which Aquinas ascribes only to angels. Recall that Homer called *nous* "the organ of clear images," and in the early Christian patristic understanding it is a spiritual organ within the heart, directly capable of apprehending God.

According to Philip Sherrard, the Thomistic view of man's spiritual capabilities is a radical departure from patristic tradition. It changes the fundamental Christian concept of man from a threefold being (*nous*, soul, and body, in the image of God's Trinity) to a twofold being, consisting of only a body and rational soul. For Sherrard, the limited twofold conception of being leaves a man bereft of his third essential spiritual dimension, which links him directly to God:

Man's sovereign faculty or organ of knowing is not the reason ... his knowledge is not confined to the sphere of the rational. He possesses in addition to the reason a supra-rational faculty or organ [*nous*], one through which he is capable of entering into direct communion with the divine ... He may know things, including himself, by knowing how they are in God. He is not ... simply a two-fold being, of soul and body, but he is a threefold being, of whom the third component—this supra-rational, more than human faculty—is as it were the spiritual subject, a seed or germ of spiritual awareness dwelling in the soul and illuminating the soul while not being identified with it.[137]

Certainly, one of the contributing factors in the loss of the early patristic teachings on the centrality of the heart and the *nous* was a lack of adequate translations. Thomas Aquinas, like Blessed Augustine, had little working knowledge of Greek. Could it be that some of the basic teachings on the *nous* and the centrality of the heart in spiritual perception were lost in translation to the Latin? Aquinas himself confirms this possibility:

Many things which sound well enough in Greek do not perhaps sound well in Latin. Hence, Latins and Greeks professing the same faith do so using different words ... It is, therefore, the task of the good translator, *when translating material dealing with the Catholic faith, to preserve the meaning, but to adapt the mode of expression so that it is in harmony with the idiom of the language into which he is translating* [emphasis added] ... [W]hen anything expressed in one language is translated merely word for word into another, it will be no surprise if perplexity concerning the meaning of the original sometimes occurs.[138]

Whether lost in translation or obscured through other historical factors, the original patristic teaching on the *nous* dwindled in the Christian West. The reason became a valid instrument for the discovery of not merely a natural and relative truth but even divine and absolute truth.[139] While the truths of revelation continued to be regarded as absolute, they were moved beyond man's capability to be fully understood or directly experienced.[140] Is it any wonder that Christians in the West and East came to misunderstand each other? A chasm had developed between the noetic and rationalistic approach to Christian spiritual perception. An ideological confrontation of these two schools of thought occurred in the fourteenth century, which came to be known as the Hesychast Controversy. St Gregory Palamas, Bishop of Thessalonica, wrote a defense for the practice of *hesychia*, "stillness," the effectiveness of which was questioned by his contemporary, the monk and philosopher Barlaam the Calabrian.[141] Barlaam's position, true to the Thomistic view, was that "the noblest part of man, through the help of which one can attain the knowledge of God, is reason."[142] He believed that "God was identical with His essence, and there was no real possibility for man to be in communion with divine essence."[143]

While the Palamite defense prevailed in the East, the Barlaamite view of spiritual perception is still generally accepted in the West. For example, Mortimer Adler writes in his Introduction to *The Gateway to Great Books*:

> Theology has two branches: the dogmatic and the natural. ... Dogmatic theology is the explication of the articles of faith; it belongs wholly to religion proper, and draws upon reason only to reach conclusions from premises established by the Word of God. But natural theology rests

wholly upon reason [emphasis added]. It may serve faith; in any case, reason must reach the same conclusions as faith (though it may not go as far) if faith is taken to be true; in the religious view, faith and the *power* of reason both proceed from God, being perfect, is without falsehood or contradiction. But the problems of natural theology are in no sense whatever dogmatic. They are independent of religion, and they are studied and argued by men of all religions and of none.[144]

In other words, one can use pure reason in arguments regarding theological questions, even without being religious. This illustrates the inherent dangers of strictly logical conceptualizations of the ontological, divorced from direct apprehension through the heart/*nous*, our organ of spiritual discernment. They tend to encourage a limited understanding of God.

There are current voices in the Christian West that now speak more openly about the possibility of deification and *theosis*. This is discussed further in a future chapter. In Dostoevsky's time, however, the noetic/rationalistic distinction was categorical. His short story "The Dream of a Ridiculous Man" squarely directs our attention to man's noetic capabilities in accordance with the early patristic teachings of the Church.

PART II

The *Nous* and Dostoevsky

CHAPTER 8

Biographical Details

A few details about Fyodor Dostoevsky's life will help set the background for the analysis of the *nous*/heart in his short story, "The Dream of a Ridiculous Man." The author's familiarity with Eastern Orthodox spirituality is intimately tied to his family roots. Biographer Joseph Frank describes the Russian aristocracy of the nineteenth century as minimally concerned with matters of their Christian Orthodoxy, although "they continued to baptize their children in the state religion and to structure their lives in accordance with its rituals."[145] However, the Dostoevsky family was a notable exception to this tendency. Dostoevsky himself attests to how pious his family was and how the Gospel's sacred stories were well known by him from early childhood.[146] He was particularly impressed with the book of Job.[147] A deacon came to their house regularly to instruct the children in their faith. According to Frank: "The attempt of theologians to rationalize the mysteries of faith … never held any appeal for Dostoevsky. What stirred his feelings to the depths was the story of the Advent as a divine-human narrative full of character and action—as an account of real people living and responding with passion and fervor to the word of God."[148] Dostoevsky was born in Moscow, and the family often visited the cathedrals within the fortress of the Kremlin, where national and religious elements blended into one.[149] They made yearly pilgrimages to the Holy Trinity Monastery founded by Saint Sergius, one of Russia's most well-known and revered saints.[150]

Dostoevsky's thoughts on the significance of the heart developed early. In adolescence, one of his favorite novels was *Сердце и думка* (*Serdtse i dumka: Heart and Head*) by Alexander Veltman. During Fyodor's student years at the military academy, his brother Mikhail writes to him: "To *know* more, one must *feel* less." Dostoevsky strongly disagrees: "What do you mean by the word *to know?* … To know nature, the soul, God, love. … These are known by the heart, not the mind."[151] The author maintained this conviction throughout his lifetime.

Unlike many of his contemporaries who immersed themselves solely in European literature, Dostoevsky was thoroughly familiar with the writings of Russian historians and poets such as Karamzin and Pushkin. His education at the Academy of Military Engineers included a humanistic education: familiarity with French and German literature of the Romantic era. He was particularly affected by the plays of Friedrich von Schiller[152] and philosopher Friedrich Schelling. Biographer Frank notably states: "Dostoevsky was influenced by Schelling's view that the highest truths were closed to discursive reason but accessible by a superior faculty of 'intellectual intuition.'"[153] As one can see from this quote, Schelling may have been reaching out for, but not quite grasping, a concept similar to the Eastern Orthodox *nous*.

A great calamity occurred to Dostoevsky at the age of twenty-eight. He was sentenced to death by firing squad for participating in the Petrashevsky Circle, a radical group that pressed for the liberation of serfs in Russia.[154] Just minutes before the execution was to take place, the sentence was revoked. Instead, Dostoevsky was sent to a hard labor camp in Siberia, which he described as being confined in a coffin for four years.[155] During this time, the only book available to him was the Bible.[156] Dostoevsky came out of this experience a changed man:

> As a result, Dostoevsky's previous "secular" Christianity underwent a crucial metamorphosis. Hitherto it had been dedicated to the improvement of life on earth; now this aim, without being abandoned, became overshadowed by an awareness of the importance of the hope of eternity as a mainstay of moral existence. ... [T]he four years he spent in the prison camp were responsible for "the regeneration of his convictions" on a more mundane level. This was a result of his growing awareness of the deep roots of traditional Christianity even in the worst of peasant criminals, who bowed down during the Easter service, with a clanking of chains, when the priest read the words "accept me, O Lord, even as the thief." The basis of Dostoevsky's later faith in what he considered the ineradicable Christian essence of the Russian people arose from such experiences.[157]

Dostoevsky's childhood religious impressions now merge with a firsthand knowledge of suffering, both through his own imprisonment and exile, and through the observation of the plight of his fellow man. His Christian faith becomes much more profound. Through his ordeal, he acquires a treasure of experience which will help create the unforgettable characters of this stories and novels.

Dostoevsky was often persecuted by those in his own profession, authors and editors.[158] Most of his life he lived in poverty, giving much of what he earned to the surviving family of his dead brother and his own demanding stepson, Paul.[159] Because of constant debts he developed a passion for gambling.[160] His second marriage to Anna Grigorievna was a happy one, but marred by the infant deaths of two of his four children. Dostoevsky's visit to the Optina Monastery after the death of his three-year-old son Alyosha in 1878 had a profound influence on his spiritual understanding. At the time he met up with Elder Ambrose, who supervised the translation and editing of the Greek fathers such as those of St Paisius (Velichkovsky) and encouraged the revival of the hesychastic tradition.[161] Dostoevsky left the monastery greatly consoled, and Elder Ambrose's character clearly influenced the author's portrayal of Father Zosima in *The Brothers Karamazov*.

Besides the aforementioned woes, Dostoevsky suffered from epilepsy for many years; toward the end of his life he had severe emphysema.[162] Recognition for his literary genius came just prior to his death. Thus, when the author writes about suffering and the seeming ridiculous, he often speaks from personal experience. He writes to his older brother Mikhail in the winter of 1847:

> I am ready to give my life for you and yours, but sometimes, when my heart is full of love, you can't get a kind word out of me. My nerves don't obey me at such moments. I am ridiculous and disgusting, and I always suffer from the unjust conclusions drawn about me. People say that I am callous and without a heart. ... I can show that I am a man with a heart and love only when *external circumstances themselves, accidents,* jolt me forcibly out of my usual nastiness.[163]

Note Dostoevsky's repeated references to the heart when disclosing his true inner state. What humble words from a truly great author!

CHAPTER 9

"The Dream of a Ridiculous Man": Synopsis and Analysis of the Story

THE DORMANT *NOUS*

An unnamed protagonist is the main character of this tale; all others are only marginally involved and barely mentioned. There are brief encounters with others: an engineer and two other friends, and a momentary incident with a crying child. No direct conversation is presented: the ridiculous man simply describes the gist of his verbal exchanges. Within the context of the dream, the man meets a dark and unknown being; their conversation is likewise minimal. In the paradisiacal new earth of his dream the man meets many of its inhabitants, but their dialogue is not recounted. Dostoevsky deliberately avoids conversations and interactions in order to direct all of our attention to the inner life of the ridiculous man: only what the author's unnamed protagonist experiences, only what he thinks is significant.

"The Dream of a Ridiculous Man" is narrated in the first person. The protagonist introduces himself in the opening words:

> I am a ridiculous man. They call me a madman now. That would be a distinct rise in my social position were it not

that they still regard me as being as ridiculous as ever. But that does not make me angry any more. They are all dear to me now, even while they laugh at me—yes, even then they are for some reason particularly dear to me.[164]

He asserts that now he knows the *truth* and how difficult it is for him to be the only one who knows it. The truth in his case is a direct spiritual revelation to the eye of his soul, the organ of discernment that is termed the *nous*. He has directly experienced the divine, and it has wrought a complete change in his perception of reality and in his behavior. The authenticity of his experience is confirmed by the warmth of love he now feels for others, in place of his former cold disdain.

The term "ridiculous" may not be an adequate translation of the Russian "смешной," used by Dostoevsky. It may be more accurately rendered "peculiar," a man who is a "social misfit." He is conscious of his oddity from the very beginning, from about seven years of age on. It hurts him at first that he is ridiculous, and he tries hard to hide this from everyone, an attempt that only causes him to withdraw further and further into himself. He begins to lose touch with others, with reality. At the same time, he becomes increasingly proud. To confess to anyone that he is absurd seems an impossibility: "I do believe that if ever I had by chance confessed it to anyone, I should have blown out my brains the same evening."[165] From inner misery and alienation a profound sense of purposelessness envelops the man. At first nothing in the present seems to touch him; then he decides that nothing that happened in the past has ever mattered, nor will anything matter in the future. One could say that at the beginning of this story, the *nous* as an organ of spiritual perception is dead within this character.

The protagonist decides to kill himself. Although he is poor, he buys an excellent revolver, loads it, and keeps it in his room. Every day for two months he suspects that he may go through with this, but the time never seems to be quite right. As he heads home for his apartment one gloomy evening in November, a twinkling star in the sky catches his attention. It seems to give him the resolve to go through with the suicide. Suddenly his thoughts are interrupted by a crying child, who is desperately demanding help for her dying mother. He rudely brushes the child off, and when she continues to implore him, he stamps his foot and shouts at her, whereupon she runs off to find help elsewhere.

This encounter with the child proves pivotal. Back in his apartment he contemplates his action. Unwittingly, he becomes conscious of the pain he has caused, and he is irritated at the fact that he feels shame. It runs contrary to his conviction that nothing in the world matters. The stirring up of his conscience is evidence that something *does* matter. One perplexed thought follows another, and the man falls asleep in his chair.

In his dream, the ridiculous man follows through with the suicide. However, he shoots into his *heart*, not his head as he had planned: "I had firmly resolved to shoot myself through my head, through the right temple, to be precise."[166] This indicates that deductive reasoning is no longer determining his actions. Through this detail Dostoevsky also points out the greater significance of the heart in spiritual insight. Within the text of the story, *prior to* the dream Dostoevsky does not mention the heart at all. Yet in the seven pages devoted to the dream and the change it brings about within the man, the heart is mentioned *twenty* times.

It must be emphasized that in Dostoevsky's Orthodox spiritual tradition, the human heart is not merely "an organ of psychological and emotional activity."[167] It is the center of a man's personhood, the place where he comes into communion with God.[168] St Macarius the Great says: "The heart governs the entire organism, and when grace gains possession of the heart, it reigns over all the thoughts and all the members, for it is there, in the heart, that the mind and all the thoughts of the soul have their seat."[169] Therefore, the mind is subservient to the heart in spiritual perception. Archbishop Luke Voyno-Yasenetsky writes: "The deepest essence of our being is perceived not through the mind, but the spirit. Self-awareness is a function of the spirit, not the mind. We come to know the action of God's grace not through the spirit of this world, but through our own spirit, which has been bestowed on us by God."[170] Such self-awareness is awakened in our protagonist.

Toward a Change of Heart

Fully conscious that he is dead, the man feels himself being carried in a closed coffin and buried. An unidentified span of time passes. He is left in the dark alone, conscious, but expecting nothing. After a time, drops of water begin to fall regularly on his eyelid. He relates that: "a deep indignation blazed up in my heart."[171] The fact that this is anger or displeasure is not necessarily negative, for any kind of feeling to be elicited from a heart or *nous* that is deadened is better than no feeling at all. It is then that his first cry to an acknowledged higher Power, albeit clothed in angry words, rings out:

> And suddenly I called (not with my voice, for I was motion-less, but with the whole of my being) upon Him who was

responsible for all that was happening to me: "Whoever Thou art, and if anything more rational exists than what is happening here, let it, I pray Thee, come to pass here too. But if Thou art revenging Thyself for my senseless act of self-destruction by the infamy and absurdity of life after death, then know that no torture that may be inflicted upon me can ever equal the contempt which I shall go on feeling in silence, though my martyrdom may last for aeons upon aeons!"[172]

This is hardly what one may regard as a real prayer; it is more of a haughty challenge. Consider this a cry for help coming from the ridiculous man's very proud heart.

Suddenly, the walls of his coffin break apart and he finds himself "caught up by some dark and unknown being."[173] Still, the sense of pride does not leave him: "I did not question the being who was carrying me: I was proud and waited. I was telling myself that I was not afraid, and I was filled with admiration at the thought that I was not afraid."[174] The fact that the man feels dislike for the being flying with him through space, though it could be an angel, also reveals the darkness within his soul, the murkiness of his *nous*. As the knowledge of an afterlife dawns upon him, he feels no joy at the prospect:

"'So there is life beyond the grave!' I thought with the curious irrelevance of a dream, but at heart I remained essentially unchanged."[175] "'If I must *be* again,' I thought, 'and live again at someone's unalterable behest, I won't be defeated and humiliated!'"[176]

At this point in the story one begins to perceive a change of heart. The man acknowledges being afraid of his companion and his heart is stung with the humiliation of this implied confession.[177] A sense of foreboding envelops him. All at once he sees a sun exactly like the one we see from our earth. Its familiarity stirs an echo in his heart and awakens it. "If that is the sun just like our sun," he asks, "where is the earth?" His companion points out the emerald colored star that they are approaching.[178] The ridiculous man suddenly becomes aware of the irresistible, poignant love he feels for the planet he has left and momentarily thinks of the child he repulsed. A "holy jealousy" glows in his heart just to think that his own earth could be repeated elsewhere. He admits to himself that he "never, never ceased to love that earth, and that on the night that he parted from it he loved it more than ever."[179] "I want, I thirst, this very minute to kiss with tears streaming down my cheeks, the one and only earth that I have left behind. I don't want; I won't accept life on any other!"[180] Even before he reaches the new planet, the protagonist's heart has come alive.

THE NOUS AWAKENS

He arrives in a world similar to his own, but "everything seemed to be bathed in the radiance of some public festival and of some great and holy triumph attained at last."[181] Even the greenery and flowers radiated love; the birds perched fearlessly on his shoulders. He was joyously greeted by the planet's inhabitants. "Never on our earth had I beheld such beauty in man. Only perhaps in our children during the first years of their life could one have found a remote, though faint reflection of this beauty."[182] The man understands that he has landed on the earth that has not yet been tarnished by the Fall and that he is encountering people who have not sinned.

The people he meets are loving and joyous: "Their faces were radiant with understanding and a serenity of mind that had reached its greatest fulfillment. Those faces were joyous; in the words and voices of these people there was a childlike gladness."[183] Our protagonist realizes that these people possess a different kind of knowledge:

> I soon realized that their knowledge was derived from, and fostered by emotions (intuitions) other than those to which we were accustomed on earth, and that their aspirations, too, were quite different. They desired nothing. They were at peace with themselves. They did not strive to gain knowledge of life as we strive to understand it, because their lives were full. But their knowledge was higher and deeper than the knowledge we derive from our science; for our science seeks to explain what life is, and strives to understand it in order to teach others how to live, while they knew how to live without science. I understood that, but I couldn't understand their knowledge.[184]

The inhabitants of this paradisiacal world have the depth of noetic understanding that supersedes simple rational thought. This way of apprehending is new for the ridiculous man, and he finds it difficult to comprehend these beings.

As time passes on the new planet, more and more vistas are opened before the protagonist, and the understanding of his heart deepens. He recollects how he could scarcely discern the significance of the solemn singing that he heard in this sinless world:

> Their songs were very simple, but they sprang straight from the heart and they touched the heart. ... While

understanding words I could never entirely fathom their meaning. It remained somehow beyond the grasp of my reason, and yet it sank unconsciously deeper and deeper into my heart.[185]

He shares with the people how on his own earth he had experienced presentiments of their world in a yearning melancholy, which at times approached insufferable sorrow. He admits that even as he hated men on earth, he felt a yearning anguish and a love for them. The presence of these innocent people made his own heart as innocent and just as theirs: "The sensation of the fullness of life left me breathless, and I worshipped them in silence."[186] What he experienced was so real to him, but a thousand times brighter and more joyful than he is able to put into words. He even says: "I will tell you a secret: perhaps it was no dream at all!"[187] implying that it could have been a direct revelation. The possibility of such a revelation is confirmed by St Gregory Palamas, who says: "He [God] appears in one way to an active man, in another to a contemplative, in another again to the man of vision. … There are numerous differences in the divine vision itself: among the prophets, some have seen God in a dream, others when awake by means of enigmas and mirrors."[188]

RETURN TO A DARKER REALITY

Dostoevsky has taken us to a paradisiacal summit, and then chooses abruptly to return us back to reality, to our own fallen world. Although the precise details are not given in the story, the protagonist teaches the inhabitants of the unfallen planet to lie, thereby corrupting their perfect world. "[T]his germ of falsity made its way into their hearts and they liked it."[189] The story is referencing serpent's temptation of Adam and Eve in paradise, the darkening of the *nous* that came with the Fall. Biographer Joseph Frank insightfully explains this as follows: "Somehow, the ridiculous man introduces [a] principle of reflexive self-consciousness and self-awareness—the ultimate psychological root of egoism—into the innocent people."[190]

Contemporary psychologist Jordan B. Peterson echoes Frank's thought. "Evil enters the world with self-consciousness,"[191] he says outright. He retells the Genesis story as the awakening of this self-awareness. "Adam and Eve became ashamed, immediately after their eyes were opened. They could see—and what they first saw was themselves. Their faults stood out. Their vulnerability was on display. ... [*they*] made themselves loincloths right away, to cover up their fragile bodies—and to protect their egos. Then they promptly skittered off and hid. In their vulnerability, now fully realized, they felt unworthy to stand before God."[192]

The purified *nous*, which fully takes delight in God's presence, was now preoccupied with disturbing thoughts about self-image.

Yet how can mere self-consciousness be a such a source of evil? According to Peterson, our own experience of humiliation and pain in this fallen world teaches us how to inflict it upon others:

> We know exactly how and where we can be hurt, and why. That is as good a definition as any of self-consciousness. We are aware of our own defencelessness, finitude and mortality. We can feel pain, and self-disgust and shame, and horror, and we know it. We know what makes us suffer. We know how dread and pain can be inflicted on us—and

that means we know exactly how to inflict it on others ...
We can terrify other people, consciously. We can hurt and
humiliate them for faults we understand only too well ...
That's the entry of the knowledge of Good and Evil into
the world.[193]

Thus, with the entry of egoism and cruelty, the paradisiacal
land of the protagonist's dream begins to resemble our own fallen
world: the shedding of blood, the defense of honor, the torture
of animals.[194] "A struggle began for separation, for isolation, for
personality (individuality), for mine and thine."[195] "When they
became guilty of crimes, they invented justice and drew up whole
codes of law in order to observe it, and to ensure the carrying out
of their laws they erected a guillotine. They only vaguely remembered what they had lost, and they would not believe that they
ever were happy and innocent."[196] The people lose their *noetic*
capability of knowing, and their consciousness is now tied firmly
to the wisdom of their fallen world. The *nous*, that which is most
divine, is suppressed and even obliterated, while the superficial,
the egotistical, and potentially cruel self gains ground. Philip
Sherrard explains such a state as a fragmentation, a duality of
consciousness that occurred within fallen human nature:

> There is in man a difference between his inmost self and
> the self with which he usually and mistakenly identifies
> himself, his everyday empirical self; and it may be this split
> in his self-awareness, and the fact that in his outer, more
> superficial empirical self he is capable of ignoring and to
> a considerable extent of becoming impervious to his inner
> self, that is the most evident symptom of that internal dis-
> location of man's being which in the Christian tradition is
> indicated by the term "Fall."[197]

As the knowledge of God gradually disappears among the people in this paradisiacal world, they begin to believe in science by means of which they hope to find wisdom, saying to themselves: "Knowledge is higher than feeling, and the consciousness of life is higher than life. Science will give us wisdom. Wisdom will reveal to us the laws. And the knowledge of the laws of happiness is higher than happiness ... and having uttered those words, each of them began to love himself better than anyone else."[198] Blessed Augustine described this situation well in the *City of God*:

> So it is that two cities have been made by two loves: the earthly city by love of self to the exclusion of God; the heavenly by love of God to the exclusion of self. The one boasts in itself, the other in the Lord. The one seeks glory from men, the other finds its greatest glory in God's witness to its conscience.[199]

What follows in Dostoevsky's short story is a retelling of the rest of human history: the development of slavery, the killing of saints and prophets, wars fought for the sake of creating a "better" world. "Men arose who began to wonder how they could all be united again, so that everybody should, without ceasing to love himself best of all, not interfere with everybody else. ... [S]cience, wisdom and the instinct of self-preservation would in the end force men at last to unite into a harmonious and intelligent society."[200] Those who stood in the way of this wisdom could be exterminated.

Here Dostoevsky is combatting various philosophies of his time: that paradise can be regained through science (Hobbes, Descartes); that Utopia is possible without divine light, without community (Rousseau); that the paradisiacal state is one of self-preservation (Hobbes, Locke). Is Dostoevsky not speaking prophetically of our age as well? Advanced technology has not brought us a sense of unity; society is more sharply divided and self-centeredness continues unabated.

The ridiculous man is distraught at the change he has brought about and longs to suffer at their hands. He becomes a Christ-like figure within their midst: "I walked among them, wringing my hands and weeping over them, but I loved them perhaps more than before when there was no sign of suffering in their faces. ... I implored them to crucify me."[201] At first the people respond by laughter, but eventually they threaten to lock him up in a madhouse. It is no longer for himself that he feels pain, but for the welfare of others. In excruciating anguish of soul, suffering for this newly fallen world, the ridiculous man awakes.

THE NOUS ENLIGHTENED

He leaps up in amazement and flings away the loaded revolver. An immeasurable ecstasy and a zest for living flood his soul. "I lifted up my hands and called upon eternal Truth—no, not called upon it, but wept."[202] He wants to live and spread the good tidings of what he has learned, no matter what others think of him. He knows with every fiber of his being that he has seen the truth:

> I have seen it and I know that people can be happy and beautiful without losing their ability to live on earth. ... I have beheld it—the Truth—it is not as though I invented it with my mind: I have beheld it, and the *living image* of it has filled my soul forever. I have beheld it in all its glory and I cannot believe that it cannot exist among men. ...

The main thing is to love your neighbor as yourself—that is the main thing, and that is everything, for nothing else matters.[203]

The most powerful idea of the story, the Gospel truth, has thus been stated. As the Father loved Me, I also have loved you; abide [continue] in My love. ... This is My commandment, that you love one another as I have loved you" (John 15:9, 12). In conclusion, Dostoevsky (through his protagonist) reiterates his commitment to fight the notion that "the consciousness of life is higher than life, the knowledge of happiness is higher than happiness."[204] In direct contrast to the beginning of the story, the ridiculous man, his *nous* now enlightened, runs to find the hurt child that he had so rudely rejected the night before. His heart is now full of love and compassion. The story ends with the words: "And I shall go on!"[205]—a confirmation of his belief in eternal life.

Here is how Ivan Ilyin describes religious transformation, akin to what has transpired with our protagonist:

Religious perception is a true spiritual event, which not only captures the deepest source of one's personal strength—it occurs precisely within that depth ... This penetration may be instantaneous or gradual, "transforming" or "rebuilding"; ... it is characterized by decisiveness and determination. If the depth of this soul is so enkindled, the divine sparks and rays will envelop it entirely ... the divine experience becomes absolutely real, everything else pales in comparison, becomes secondary, doubtful ... even illusory.[206]

With his artistic pen Dostoevsky has drawn two portraits of the same individual: one before his spiritual awakening and a very different one after his encounter with the truth. The former man is a gloomy, proud, and miserable individual whose life makes no sense, whose isolation leads him to seek suicide; the reformed man is repentant, yet joyous, life-loving, and purposeful. He still seems ridiculous to those around him, but this no longer hurts him. People have grown dear to him, and he only regrets that they lack the knowledge of the truth that has been revealed so clearly to him by his dream. He longs to share this personal experience of direct contact with the divine that has purified his heart but lacks adequate words, for what has been revealed to his heart or *nous* is beyond worldly description. What he knows now is the capability of "man's unity in love according to Christ's testament."[207]

Is this not reminiscent of Plato's allegory of the Cave, where the man whose *nous* has been illumined returns to retrieve those in darkness, so that they may likewise be enlightened? Yet they do not listen to him, for in their darkness he is unintelligible to them. They even dare to kill him.

How well has Dostoevsky's "The Dream of a Ridiculous Man" illustrated St Gregory Palamas's words: "The heart of man is the controlling organ, the throne of grace. The *nous* and all the thoughts of the soul are to be found there."[208] He shows how a suicidal man's stony heart, full of pride and self-love, can be converted to a heart/*nous* that is able to directly perceive and reflect God's love and reach its divine potential.

CHAPTER 10

Examples of Other "Ridiculous Men" in Dostoevsky's Novels

One may wonder why Dostoevsky typically chooses the misfits and those who are somehow ridiculous to illustrate the inner workings of the heart and the *nous*. A possible explanation is the tension between the sin of pride and the virtue of humility within every human being. Persons with a dormant, darkened *nous* will typically feel indignant and angry if they are labeled ridiculous, whether they have determined this for themselves or have been seen that way by others. Once the *nous* is awakened and God's law takes precedence within the heart, the attitude of others matters less. One's ridiculousness is no longer so relevant and important. Self-consciousness takes a backseat.

Thus, the characters that Dostoevsky endows with an enlightened *nous* tend not to fit well into their worldly environments, just as the nameless protagonist of our short story. They are Dostoevsky's true heroes and to them he grants experiences of sudden spiritual revelation. Alongside the heroes one finds his antiheroes, those with a darkened *nous*.

This author is especially adept at illustrating an individual's inner struggle, whose *nous* alternatively experiences light and darkness. According to translator David Magarshack, herein lies the genius of Dostoevsky as a writer:

> Through the mind and heart of the characters he created, he could reach out beyond the borderlines of conscious thought into the darkest recesses of the human personality and, at the same time, provide the deepest analysis of human nature and human destiny that any creative writer before or after him was ever able to achieve.[209]

According to Magarshack, Dostoevsky's short stories are able to reflect "the highest expression of his creative power and profundity of thought. In these smaller works we find reflected as in a convex mirror the whole immensity of Dostoevsky's world, concentrated with gem-like brilliance and startling clarity."[210] We have found just such a concentration of Christian philosophic thought in "The Dream of a Ridiculous Man." And we will see that Dostoevsky remains true to his philosophy within the idiom of his longer works. This chapter highlights Prince Myshkin and Parfyon Rogozhin of *The Idiot*, Alyosha Karamazov and Markel, Elder Zosima's brother in *The Brothers Karamazov*, and the formidable Nikolai Stavrogin in *Demons*.

It is within this tension of the battle between good and evil that Dostoevsky's characters come alive, destined to become negative or positive according to the openness of their *nous* to the perception of God. Saint Justin Popovich[211] elaborates upon this in his book, *The Philosophy and Religion of F. M. Dostoevsky:*

> The affirmative or negative resolution of eternal questions predetermines a man's entire life, his philosophy and religion, his morality and reason for living—this is a basic premise for Dostoevsky. The negative resolution of this

problem, as exemplified by the words: "there is no God, no immortality" creates the essence of Dostoevsky's negative characters; the affirmative solution: "there is a God, there is immortality" creates the essence of his positive characters … Love is the practical manifestation of the perception of God and the confirmation of one's personal immortality. The souls of Dostoevsky's positive characters are woven of such perceptions; because of this their life reflects a beautiful tapestry woven by God. Their hearts are filled with God and immortality. Everything which exudes from them is divine and eternal. If there is a God, and if there is immortality, then authentic love is a real possibility. Without [God] it is a psychological and ontological impossibility.[212]

PRINCE LEV MYSHKIN OF *THE IDIOT*

The very title of the novel, *The Idiot*, gives us the first clue as to the oddity of its main character, Prince Lev Myshkin. From the very first train ride, during which the Prince meets his adversary, the passionate Parfyon Rogozhin, Myshkin's appearance and mannerisms suggest how little he fits into society. "His eyes were big, blue and intent; their gaze had something quiet but heavy about it and was filled with a strange expression by which some are able to guess at first sight that the subject has the falling sickness."[213] In fact, it is during an epileptic fit later in the novel that Myshkin seems to catch a glimpse of the beauty of another world, reminiscent of the dream in Dostoevsky's short story:

He fell to thinking, among other things, about his epileptic condition, that there was a stage in it just before the fit itself, when suddenly, amidst the sadness, the darkness of soul, the pressure, his brain would momentarily catch fire, as it were, and all his life's forces would be strained at once in an extraordinary impulse. The sense of life, of self-awareness, increased nearly tenfold in these moments, which flashed by like lightning. His mind, his heart were lit up with an extraordinary light; all his agitation, all his doubts, all his worries were as if placated at once, resolved in a sort of sublime tranquility, filled with serene, harmonious joy and hope, filled with reason and ultimate cause.[214]

In the course of the first conversation, Rogozhin and his companion laugh at Prince Myshkin, because he is so open in answering personal questions. They are amazed at his calm assertion that he has no idea where he will be staying in St Petersburg.[215] Myshkin has a rare talent for acting from the heart and lacks the social graces of high society. Dostoevsky accounts this a positive characteristic, for he presents most of high society conversation as hypocritical, bourgeois politeness. In contrast to the socially accepted behavior that surrounds him, the Prince speaks with an almost naive, frank openness, first to the lackey of General Epanchin and then to the Epanchin family.[216] Similarly, he does not hesitate to publicly reveal his admiration for Nastasya Filippovna when he arrives uninvited to her home: "Everything in you is perfection … even the fact that you're so thin and pale … one has no wish to imagine you otherwise … I wanted so much to come to you. … I … forgive me."[217] Throughout the course of the novel, Prince Myshkin is sometimes admired, but most often he is openly ridiculed.

From the introduction to the novel we learn that in the character of Prince Myshkin Dostoevsky was attempting to portray a positively beautiful man, even a Christ-like figure. He realized how difficult a task this would be. In a letter to his friend Maikov, he speaks of his creative process: "In my head and in my soul many artistic conceptions flash and make themselves felt. But they only flash; and what's needed is a full embodiment, which always comes about unexpectedly and suddenly … then, once you have received the full image in your heart, you can set about its artistic realization."[218] Thus, the raw material of his imagination was given the greatest freedom and he "never imposed an ideological resolution on his work."[219]

Inevitably, character flaws of the positively beautiful Prince Myshkin are revealed. Though Christ-like in some ways, he is a human being after all. As the novel unfolds, the Prince becomes more and more reticent; his humility and meekness work against him. It is his heart that gets him into trouble, for it is divided between his two loves, Nastasya Filippovna and Aglaya Epanchin. Through his lack of discernment between true love and pity,[220] he is unable to choose and falls back into the sickness that afflicted him prior to the opening of the novel.

There is a particular aspect of the novel, *The Idiot*, that relates directly to our study of *nous* and the heart. According to Olga Meerson, "Dostoevsky uses the language of social interactions for non-social purposes … in order to depict and address human conscience, conscious, unconscious, subconscious."[221] In other words, just as in his short story, Dostoevsky is looking at the *inner soul* of his characters. Dostoevsky places the naive idealist Prince Myshkin (a man with a relatively passion-free, enlightened *nous*) in opposition to the lustful and passion-driven Parfyon Rogozhin (one with a darkened *nous*) throughout the novel. Is this merely to illustrate two different states of the heart? According to translator Richard Pevear, the final scene of the novel—which finds the two of them together, pressed face to face—suggests that the author has created an image of the contrasts and battles that may go on within a single soul: "Dostoevsky's doubles, which might seem images of personal division, are in fact images of human oneness."[222] Philip Sherrard offers a similar thought: "Man is in some way double in himself. There is a Cain and Abel within him. Indeed, the Cain in him—his superficial ego—is even capable of denying and so of metaphorically killing the real source of his being, his own inner depths, the Abel in him."[223]

ALYOSHA KARAMAZOV OF *THE BROTHERS KARAMAZOV*

In Dostoevsky's most famous novel *The Brothers Karamazov*, the youngest of these brothers, Alyosha, can also be considered "ridiculous." In his case it mostly means "other-worldly," even Christ-like in the sense that Prince Myshkin was. As Dostoevsky describes him: "Alyosha was not at all a fanatic, and in my view at least, even not at all a mystic. I will give my full opinion beforehand: he was simply an early lover of mankind. ... However, I do not deny that he was, at that time, already very strange, having been so from the cradle."[224]

Alyosha frequented the local Russian Orthodox monastery because of his filial love for the Elder Zosima. It is following the death of his cherished teacher that one significant incident occurs. A short time after the elder passes away, an odor of corruption issues from the coffin.[225] This causes Elder Zosima's enemies to greatly rejoice, for they believe that this negates his sanctity. Alyosha's young heart is wrenched with the pain of both losing his beloved teacher and the elder's seeming disgrace. His first instinct is to run away from the monastery, but he returns to the elder's coffin.[226] He hears the Gospel account of the *Marriage of Cana* being read over the deceased. At that point Alyosha falls asleep and in a dream sees Elder Zosima among the guests at the Lord's banquet. This assures him of Father Zosima's righteousness, confirms him in his faithful respect and love for the elder, and in God's mercy. Dostoevsky describes Alyosha's moments after his awakening: "Something burned in Alyosha's *heart* [emphasis added], something suddenly filled him almost painfully, tears of rapture nearly burst from his soul."[227] He runs outside to embrace the world:

> Alyosha stood gazing and suddenly, as if he had been cut down, threw himself to the earth.
>
> He did not know why he was embracing it, he did not try to understand why he longed so irresistibly to kiss it, to kiss all of it. But he was kissing it weeping, sobbing and watering it with his tears, and he vowed ecstatically to love it, to love it unto ages of ages. "Water the earth with the tears of your joy, and love those tears …" rang in his soul. What was he weeping for? Oh! in his rapture he wept even for the stars that shone on him from the abyss, and "he was not ashamed of that ecstasy." It was as if threads from all those innumerable worlds of God all came together in his soul, and it was trembling all over, "touching other worlds." He wanted to forgive everyone and for everything, and to ask forgiveness, oh, not for himself! but for all and for everything, "as others are asking for me," rang again in his soul. But with each moment he felt clearly and almost tangibly something as firm and immovable as this heavenly vault descend into his soul. Some sort of idea, as it were, was coming to reign in his

mind—now for the whole of his life and unto ages of ages. He fell to the earth a weak youth and rose up a fighter, steadfast for the rest of his life, and he knew and felt it suddenly at the very moment of his ecstasy. Never, never in all his life would Alyosha forget that moment. "Someone visited my soul in that hour," he would say afterwards, with firm belief in his words.[228]

Here is yet another example of a life-changing moment, a profound revelation to the *nous*/heart. We hear an echo of this incident in "The Dream of a Ridiculous Man," where the protagonist expresses fervent love for our world: "I long, I thirst, this very instant, to kiss with tears the earth that I have left, and I don't want, I won't accept life on any other!"[229] St Gregory Palamas writes that a manifestation of a cured *nous* is the attainment of real love, when "you pray to the Lord in compunction and sweet pain equally for yourself and for every person, known and unknown, enemy and friend."[230] Alyosha may have felt the intensity of this love for only a few brief moments, but it changed his life. Similarly, the protagonist in "The Dream" also experienced that intensity of love for all, for he says: "The main thing is to love your neighbor as yourself—that is the main thing, and that is everything, for nothing else matters."[231]

MARKEL, ELDER ZOSIMA'S BROTHER, IN *THE BROTHERS KARAMAZOV*

There is another short but significant passage regarding a dramatic spiritual change in the novel *The Brothers Karamazov*. Within Alyosha's biographical account of Father Zosima, the elder recounts the final days of his older brother, Markel, who had never been religious. At seventeen years of age, Markel fell under the influence of an exiled freethinker, who further confirmed him in his atheism.[232] Shortly thereafter, Markel became sick with galloping consumption and the doctors gave him less than a year to live. His mother convinces him to go to church to take Confession and Holy Communion—which he does, but only for the sake of pleasing her.[233] Soon after this an utter change in spirit comes over Markel; he is filled with an inner joy as with light. He tells his mother: "Do not weep, life is paradise, and we are all in paradise, but we do not want to know it, and if we did want to know it, tomorrow there would be paradise the world over."[234] He also begins to exhibit great tenderness and love for everyone, including the servants: "My beloved, my dear ones, why do you serve me, am I worthy of being served? If God were to have mercy on me and let me live I would begin serving you."[235] He expresses a thought so characteristic of Dostoevsky—that each of us is responsible for one another's sins: "Verily each one of us is guilty before everyone, for everyone and everything. I do not know how to explain it to you, but I feel it so strongly that it pains me."[236] Markel even asks forgiveness of the birds. The physician caring for him regards this as madness from the sickness. Thus, Markel, too, has become a ridiculous man.

Here we see the essence of a "negative-turned-positive character" in Dostoevsky. Just as in "The Dream of a Ridiculous Man," the formerly darkened *nous* of a young atheist is enlightened and an unexpected but dramatic change occurs. Markel read no books to change his mind: he simply encountered holiness through the sacraments of the Church, and a divine illumination was given to his heart.

NIKOLAI STAVROGIN IN *DEMONS*

A very different characterization of the ridiculous is presented in Nikolai Stavrogin of the novel *Demons*. Dostoevsky describes his character's appearance and demeanor:

> He was not very talkative, was elegant without exquisiteness, surprisingly modest, and at the same time bold and confident like no one else among us ... . I was also struck by his face: his hair was somehow too black, his light eyes were somehow too calm and clear, his complexion was somehow too delicate and white, his color somehow too bright and clean, his teeth like pearls, his lips like coral— the very image of beauty, it would seem, and at the same time repulsive, as it were.[237]

His strangeness manifests itself soon enough: "the beast suddenly showed his claws."[238] When one respectable gentleman of the local club uses the aphorism "they won't lead me by the nose," Stavrogin grabs the man by the nose and drags him several feet across the room. This is only the first of other acts of impropriety. There is a decided prideful air about Stavrogin, and he does not seem to feel any regret for these defiant acts.[239]

Stavrogin reappears in the novel four years later and his eccentricities continue. We never learn about the full truth of Stavrogin's character until the Appendix, which describes his visit to Bishop Tikhon at a monastery on the outskirts of town.[240] During the visit he shows the bishop a letter he intends to publicize; it is a confession of his many crimes and a revealing description of his inner world: "Every extremely shameful, immeasurably humiliating, mean, and, above all, ridiculous position I have happened to get into in my life has always aroused in me, along with boundless wrath, an unbelievable pleasure … It was not the meanness that I loved but I liked the intoxication from the tormenting awareness of my baseness."[241] Bishop Tikhon reads the letter. What follows is a most profound conversation on the nature of repentance and forgiveness. What shocks Nikolai most, however, is Bishop Tikhon's observation that following the publication of the confession Stavrogin will seem ridiculous, that "the laughter will be universal."[242] "Show me, then, precisely what makes me ridiculous in my manuscript?" Nikolai demands. His pride cannot tolerate appearing ridiculous to others.

Stavrogin is striving to forgive himself and desires to suffer humiliation from those who will learn of his crimes. Yet Bishop Tikhon questions the sincerity of his repentance, for he sees that Stavrogin is still expressing hatred for those who will read the letter.[243] "Even the form of this truly great repentance has something ridiculous in it. … [I]t has always been that the most disgraceful cross becomes a great glory and a great power, if the humility of the deed is sincere."[244] He suggests to Stavrogin that he not publicize the letter but that he secretly place himself in obedience to an obscure elder for five to seven years, without taking monastic vows, and quietly work on sincere repentance. Stavrogin leaves in a huff; the demonic spirit within him wins, driving him to suicide.

In the character of Nikolai Stavrogin, Dostoevsky has painted for us a sinister portrait of a man with a darkened *nous*, a man whose passions have full control of his life. The principal passion within Stavrogin is pride, which defies his attempts at repentance. In this he resembles the ridiculous man in our short story who was immeasurably proud and ready to kill himself because people laughed at him. Bishop Tikhon appears to have been sent into Stavrogin's life as a final appeal to follow the intuition of his heart—to sincerely repent of his past and make a new beginning. In contrast to the ridiculous man of our short story, Stavrogin loses the battle of good and evil within his *nous* and hangs himself. We learn that a humble, repentant state is essential for the salvation of a human soul and how pride leads to perdition.

PART III

The *Nous* in Contemporary Thought

CHAPTER 11

References to the Unnamed *Nous*

The reasons for the gradual decline in noetic perception in the West were discussed in detail in Part I, Chapter 7. Following the Augustinian-Thomistic model, the Greek term *nous*, derived primarily from Aristotelian philosophical texts, was translated as *intellectus* into Latin. This was not the deiform[245] ontological receptor within the heart capable of directly participating in the divine (deification, *theosis*) as seen by the early Greek fathers, but a superior mental faculty of the soul that could analogically conceptualize God as the cause of our natural, sensible world. Moreover, the word *mind* replaced the word *nous* in sacred and secular texts, changing its meaning, for the term "mind" suggests that man's understanding of the spiritual may be limited to a form of rational thinking.

However, since *nous* is universal to all human beings, it has continued to manifest itself within the works of great authors of Western literature, even when is not identified as such. One can call this phenomenon "the unnamed *nous*." The first clue of its presence comes in statements that note that spiritual perception often exceeds intellectual prowess, that there is an experiential component to spiritual existence that cannot logically be explained. Here are just a few examples:

JOSEF PIEPER (1904–1997)

Josef Pieper, in his insightful book *Leisure: The Basis of Culture*, speaks of a distinction that existed in the Middle Ages between *ratio* and *intellectus*:

> The Middle Ages drew a distinction between the understanding as *ratio* and the understanding as *intellectus*. Ratio is the power of discursive, logical thought, of searching and of examination, of abstraction, of definition and drawing conclusions. *Intellectus*, on the other hand, is the name for the understanding in so far as it is the capacity of *simplex intuitus*, of that *simple vision to which truth offers itself like a landscape to the eye* [emphasis added]. The faculty of mind, man's knowledge, is both these things in one … it is the ratio, they held, which is distinctively human; the *intellectus* they regarded as being already beyond the sphere allotted to man. And yet it belonged to man, though in one sense "superhuman"; the "purely human" by itself could not satiate man's powers of comprehension, for man, of his very nature, reaches out beyond the sphere of the human, touching on the order of pure spirits.[246]

Pieper's emphasis on this historical distinction between *ratio* and *intellectus* echoes the patristic understanding of *nous*, for it suggests that human intuition is indeed capable of noetic understanding, akin to the angels, who possess perfect knowledge of intelligible truth.

MARTIN HEIDEGGER (1889–1976)

Although this famous twentieth-century German philosopher severed his ties to Roman Catholicism early in life, he is relevant to our discussion of *nous* in his profound nostalgia for the vocabulary and understanding of life in ancient Greece. According to this philosopher, the Greek and German tongues are the most powerful and most spiritual of all languages.[247] The translation all of Greek philosophical language into Latin signaled "the first stage in the isolation and alienation of the originary essence of Greek philosophy."[248] For Heidegger it was in ancient Greece, in the poetic tragedies of Sophocles,[249] in the philosophy of Parmenides and Heraclitus[250] that authentic being was manifest. The term the Greeks used for this was *phusis*. The English definition of this word is "an unfolding that opens itself up, that holds sway … *Phusis* is Being itself, by virtue of which beings first become and remain observable."[251] According to Heidegger, the translation of *phusis* into the Latin *natura* destroyed the "philosophic authentic naming force"[252] of the Greek word. This hearkens back to our discussion in Part I, Chapter 7, on how the Platonic worldview was gradually replaced by the more concrete, categorical outlook of Aristotle.

Heidegger gives other examples of loss of original meaning in translation from Greek to Latin. The Greek word *ousia*, which originally means "being" in the sense of constant presence becomes *substantia* in Latin, something more material and limited.[253] He likewise says that the Greek concept of apprehension (*noein*), changed to a Latinized "logos," loses depth in translation. *Logos* in its original meaning was a revealing gathering, whereas in the Aristotelian sense, "logos" is an assertion of what can be true or false. "In becoming a property of assertion, truth

(*aletheia*) does not just shift its place; it changes its essence. ...
Truth becomes the correctness of logos."[254] Heidegger claims
that such a scholastic approach to the concept of being led Western philosophy into a profound misunderstanding of the Greek
terms—*logos, aletheia, phusis, noein*—for two millennia.[255] Perhaps without realizing it, this philosopher is grieving for the loss
of the authentic meaning of *nous* in Western culture, at least in
terms of how it was understood in ancient Greece.

William F. Lynch (1908–1987)

We have seen that Dostoevsky himself uses the idiom of fiction
to impart the spiritual significance of *nous*. In his book *Christ
and Apollo: The Dimensions of the Literary Imagination*, William
Lynch states: "The laws of the human *ratio*, or reason are not
the total laws of the actual; the two can never be *wholly* identical. ... Not for nothing has the human 'reason' been called *ratio
ambumbrata*, the reason of shadows."[256] This leads one to search
for parallels to the *nous* in his thinking. William Lynch's tool
to explore metaphysical phenomena is the *literary imagination*,
through the direct action of which one can pass beyond the limits of our simple and limited humanity.[257]

It is not surprising that Lynch chooses to cite passages from
the literary works of Fyodor Dostoevsky. *What* he chooses
to cite is significant, for it matches those passages that were
quoted in this book earlier: Prince Lev Myshkin's perception of intense beatitude just prior to an epileptic fit in *The
Idiot*;[258] Alyosha's rapture and sense of harmony following his
dream of the Wedding at Cana in *The Brothers Karamazov*;[259]
and Stavrogin's meeting with Bishop Tikhon in *Demons*, also
known as *The Possessed*.[260] When describing the scene in *The*

Brothers Karamazov at the monastery following the death of Elder Zosima, Lynch notes:

> He [Dostoevsky] is about to use the trivial matter [the fact that men love the downfall and disgrace of the righteous] as an instrument for the exploration of various individuals' hearts and ideas. I count fourteen such explorations within a few pages, and the importance of the total must not be minimized, for each heart, though different from that of all the other actors on the scene, serves to illuminate every other, and all serve to illuminate the counter-heart of Alyosha."[261]

Through this quote, Lynch confirms the centrality of the heart (*nous*) in Dostoevsky's writing. Recall that the heart is mentioned *twenty* times in the span of seven pages in "The Dream of a Ridiculous Man."

C. S. Lewis (1898–1963)

The immensely popular Anglican apologist and fictional writer C. S. Lewis can also be included in the examples of those who write about the unnamed *nous*. At the end of his famous book *Mere Christianity*, in the chapter entitled "New Men," he discusses man's capability of deification, "a change of being creatures of God to being sons of God"[262]:

> I have called Christ the "first instance" of the new man. But of course He is something much more than that. He is not merely *a* new man, one specimen of the species, but *the* new man. He is the origin and center and life of all the new men. He came into the created universe, of His own will, bringing with Him the *Zoe*, the new life. (I mean new

to us, of course: in its own place *Zoe* had existed for ever
and ever.) And He transmits it not by heredity but by what
I have called "good infection." Everyone who gets it gets it
by personal contact with Him. Other men become "new"
by being "in Him."[263]

Lewis is repeating, albeit in a more modern way, St Athanasius's
thought that "Christ was made man that we might be made
God." In fact, in a recent reprinting of Athanasius's treatise *On
the Incarnation*, it is Lewis himself who writes the introduction.

An article in *In Pursuit of Truth: A Journal of Christian Scholarship* affirms that this idea of Lewis—a more mystical, ontological approach to spiritual perception—is central not only to his
apologetic works but throughout his fiction:

> Although largely forgotten by Christians today, deification
> is at the heart of 'Lewis' vision of reality. From his sermons
> to his apologetic essays, from his space fiction to his chil-
> dren's stories, one can hardly find a corner of his literary
> universe that is not illumined by the idea. Although schol-
> ars in recent years have begun to explore "the overlooked
> Lewis"—including his affinities with Christian mysticism
> and the details of his spiritual formation in the Church of
> England—little attention has been given to the importance
> of deification in Lewis's thought, or to its place within
> the larger constellation of his beliefs including joy, myth,
> temptation, and sacramental life.[264]

Lewis does not use the word *nous*, but, like Dostoevsky, imparts
a spiritual message about it. *Nous* is the "eye of the soul" that
is capable of deification. One lingering question remains: Can
ontological noetic perception become part of our everyday lives
or must it be limited to the literary imagination?

CHAPTER 12

A Renewed Interest in Deification

It is not only C. S. Lewis's writings in the West that center upon deification. There has been resurgence of interest in this Eastern Orthodox teaching in the last few decades. In the most recent edition of *Catechism of the Catholic Church*, the most up-to-date reference manual of Roman Catholicism, we find the following passage:

> The Word became flesh to make us "partakers of the divine nature": "For this is why the Word became man, and the Son of God became the Son of man: so that man, by entering into communion with the Word and thus receiving divine sonship, might become a son of God." "For the Son of God became man so that we might become God."
>
> "The only-begotten Son of God, wanting to make us sharers in his divinity, assumed our nature, so that he, made man, might make men gods."[265]

This is a direct acknowledgment of the early patristic teaching of the Christian Church. Pope John Paul II (1920–2005) spoke about it in May of 1995, using the term "divinization," a synonym for deification:

> In divinization and particularly in the sacraments, Eastern theology attributes a very special role to the Holy Spirit:

through the power of the Spirit who dwells in man deification already begins on earth; the creature is transfigured and God's kingdom inaugurated. The teaching of
the Cappadocian Fathers on divinization passed into the
tradition of all the Eastern Churches and is part of their
common heritage. This can be summarized in the thought
already expressed by Saint Irenaeus at the end of the second century: God passed into man so that man might pass
over to God. This theology of divinization remains one of
the achievements particularly dear to Eastern Christian
thought. On this path of divinization, those who have been
made "most Christ-like" by grace and by commitment
to the way of goodness go before us: the martyrs and the
saints. ... In order for man to become God, the Word took
on humanity.[266]

Thus, the Roman Catholic Church is no longer so categorical on
this subject as in Dostoevsky's time.

In a recently published book entitled *Theosis: Patristic Remedy for Evangelical Yearning at the Close of the Modern Age*, writer
Michael Paul Gama recalls his own journey to the Eastern Christian Church from his family roots of Roman Catholicism and
Evangelicalism. He comprehensively quotes the early Christian fathers on *theosis* and offers encouragement for "thought-
ful millennial evangelicals" who are thirsting for an authentic
encounter with God:[267] "I see ... a reason for hope ... a growing
number of serious evangelicals exploring their common heritage in the ancient, historical church."[268]

Gama cites well-known Eastern Orthodox theologians
(Vladimir Lossky, Andrew Louth) as well as Western authors
such as patristic scholar Norman Russell (*The Doctrine of*

Deification in the Greek Patristic Tradition), Professor Daniel A. Keating (*Deification and Grace*), Lutheran minister and Finnish theologian Veli-Matti Karkkainen (*One with God: Salvation as Deification and Justification*). The titles alone speak clearly of how Western theologians have embraced the patristic teaching on deification. A most telling quote from Karkkainen hearkens back to Philip Sherrard's Christian definition of man[269]: "Any religion that wants to redeem its promises should give an answer to the most profound question of human life, namely, what is the way back to God, to live in God and share in the divine?" Karkkainen follows up by answering his own question: "Christian theology from the beginning has offered an answer to the world and its followers in the form of the doctrine of deification and/or union with God."[270]

Because deification is now acknowledged and sought after by such contemporary theologians, there is hope that the heart (*nous*) can come to regain its rightful place in the discussion of authentic religious experience. Philosopher Ivan Ilyin describes its significance as follows:

> The heart is the most free element of the powers of the human spirit, not tolerating any commands or prohibitions. Religious faith burns within it with full power and answers its calling when and only when it is the manifestation of free love toward unconditional Perfection—a love which in God has found its true Object and inexhaustible source. This is the first and basic idea of Christianity—particularly in its Eastern understanding and implementation.[271]

CHAPTER 13

Contemporary Orthodox Writers
on the *Nous*

It has been my fervent desire in this book to acquaint the reader with the *nous*, the ontological receptor, with all its permutations of meaning over time and its philosophical and theological significance. Once this concept becomes familiar, it is easy to spot direct and indirect references to it, particularly in literary works of Eastern Orthodox writers who speak of intuition, the heart, inner stillness (*hesychia*) or describe a revelation of ontological truth. While *nous* is a "household term" in more serious theological literature, it is heartening to come across it in recent publications intended for laypeople as well.

Frederica Mathewes-Green, in a book entitled *Welcome to the Orthodox Church: An Introduction to Eastern Christianity*, calls the *nous* "our listening mind":

> When we ask the question: How do we experience God? the scriptural view would be that we do encounter Him by means of our mind. Not by our ability to reason, though; we do this by the means of the *listening* mind. ... In biblical Greek it is called the *nous*.[272]

She relates the experience of her own conversion to Christ as a sudden revelation of truth to her heart:

I had a dramatic conversion to Christianity; I was a young college grad and calling myself a Hindu when, as a hitch-hiking tourist in Dublin, I went into a church and stopped to look at a statue of Jesus. I suddenly heard a voice inside, speaking to me, saying; "I am your life." (It wasn't a voice I heard with my ears, but resonated inside, filling my awareness.)

When I tried to describe this to others later on, I would say that it was like there was a little radio in my heart that I had never known was there. Suddenly it snapped on and I could hear a voice inside, speaking to me. I had no doubt who it was, for our Lord speaks "with authority." (Luke 4:32)

When I ran across this little word, *nous*, many years later, I realized that it was the "little radio" I had been trying to describe. Everyone is born with the little radio; everyone is capable of hearing the voice of God. It doesn't matter whether you are a rational or emotional sort of person. God will speak to you, in any case, through your mind— your receptive, listening mind.[273]

The author supports the patristic teaching that man's *nous* has been darkened and damaged by the fall. She expresses it in more contemporary terms:

Because the *nous* is damaged, we perceive this world wrongly enough, and misunderstand ... . [We] today must live in the most unreality-saturated generation in history, with movies, video games, and superhero mythology pressing in on us from every side. Glamorous unreality makes present reality look dowdy. It will take some time and effort, some growth in self-control, to detox the *nous*.[274]

Healing the *nous* requires inner stillness, watchfulness, "perseverance in prayer, and a mental habit of being attentive to God's presence."[275] How hard this is to learn today and how much more difficult this becomes for each new technologically dependent generation!

Albert S. Rossi's book, *Becoming a Healing Presence*, also confronts the challenge of finding quietude in a noisy and distracted world. The Bible quote "Be still, and know that I am God" (Psalm 45:11 LXX/46:10) is central to this author's message. Without this inner silence, according to Rossi, we lose the sense of who we are meant to be:

> The high price for not being still is the possibility that we might not know God. If we don't know God, we don't know ourselves, because we are made in God's image and likeness. That's who we are. Hence, today many people are looking for their identity, for their place in the world, for who they are. The only place we can find who we are is in God.[276]

Rossi's chapter entitled "The Healing Heart" is replete with quotes from the Holy Fathers. Of particular interest to us is his reference to "the heart brain," a new concept coined by cardiologists in the 1990s. Rossi relates that scientists have conducted studies over several decades that show that "the physical heart is an organ of great intelligence with its own nervous system [and] decision-making powers .... The heart ... emits an energy field five thousand times stronger than the brain's, one that can be measured more than ten feet away."[277] Cutting-edge science may term this "heart-brain," but these neuro-cardiologic study results are further confirmation of the existence of the *nous*, the ontological receptor known to philosophy and theology for centuries.

A final example of contemporary writings about the *nous* comes from a recent reprint of Abbot Nikon Vorobiev's *Letters to Spiritual Children*. The expanded biographical account about the author contains a passage so similar to the excerpts of Dostoevsky's works included in this book. Nicholas Vorobiev, the future Abbot Nikon (1894–1963), loses his childhood faith in God and as a college student struggles hard to find the true meaning of life. In his case the revelation does not come effortlessly. He is close to suicide when he finally cries out from the depths of his soul: "Lord, if you exist, reveal yourself to me!" What follows is truly reminiscent of the experience of Alyosha Karamazov, Lev Myshkin, or the ridiculous man of Dostoevsky's "The Dream":

> It is impossible to convey that action of grace which convinces a person of the existence of God—with such power and clarity that there is left not the slightest doubt. The Lord reveals Himself like the sun suddenly bursts out from behind a dark cloud; here there is no doubt whether it's the sun or someone has lit a lantern. When in just such a way the Lord revealed Himself to me, I could only fall to the ground and say: "Lord, glory to Thee, I thank Thee! Grant that I might serve Thee all the days of my life! Let all manner of misfortunes and sufferings that there be here on earth fall upon me—grant that I may endure it all, only grant that I not fall away from Thee."
>
> How long this Damascus moment lasted, Nicholas did not know, but it served to change his worldview completely. Yes, it was a miracle; at the same time it was also the natural, logical culmination of his intense search.[278]

God spoke to Nicholas through his ontological receptor, the *nous*. This sudden, intuitive grasp of spiritual truth as described by characters in Dostoevsky's fiction is likewise possible in real life. Abbot Nikon's subsequent existence was full of privations and hardship, but he became a guiding light for believers. His legacy survives through his instructive letters, which stress humility above all.

From the time of the Pre-Socratic philosophers through the centuries of Christian patristic thought and even to the present, *nous*, the heart centered ontological receptor, has persistently taken part in mankind's spiritual experience of the divine.

CONCLUSION

I n his short story "The Dream of a Ridiculous Man" and within his larger novels, Dostoevsky shares a significant measure of his own profound religious experience. He draws our attention to man's heart, which is defined here more patristically as the *nous*. Tracing the *nous'* long history throughout centuries of philosophic and religious thought shows not only how important this ontological receptor has been in the past, but how relevant it should be for authentic spiritual perception in the present.

The most vital point is this: God has given mankind a capacity to reflect His holiness in a very real way. He wishes to restore the dignity of His sonship within each person. Faithful to the spirit of the Holy Fathers, Dostoevsky speaks about direct revelation to the heart (*nous*). He does this within the context of the ancient Eastern Orthodox Church, where the most complete teaching on deification is found. Within this tradition one finds accounts of a multitude of saints who labored tirelessly to purify the "eye of the soul." They did not do this on their own, but with the help of God and their spiritual fathers. In this sense, Bishop Tikhon's advice to Stavorgin in Dostoevsky's *Demons* is also applicable to those who follow the Eastern Orthodox practice: in order to make any significant progress in the purification of the *nous*, one needs the help of an experienced priest.

Dostoevsky's appeal to the heart should resonate with every Christian, indeed, with every human being. His simple story about a ridiculous man, who begins with a revolver at his temple and ends with a profound love for all of humanity, holds many lessons for us. Most of all, it gives hope. It confirms that God is within reach of all who truly call upon Him in difficult circumstances. It teaches about God's providence for every individual and His ability to reveal His power to each person at the precise moment when he needs it most, and in a way that he can understand it best. It shows how significantly one can be changed by a single encounter with His divine goodness. Moreover, it points out where to look for sanctity: namely, in those who have opened up their heart (*nous*) to God to the extent that they themselves have become transfigured by Christ and shine with the ineffable Light of Mount Tabor. It is made apparent by their Christ-like love for all of creation, their profound sense of responsibility and care for man and beast. And may it be truly humbling to know how often most of us fall short of this Christ-like ideal.

Bishop Nikolai (Velimirovich) of Serbia tells this story in one of his missionary letters:

> You write to me of a pious visitor who began to preach to the people about the great mercy of God and the hardness of heart of sinners. Tears ran down his cheeks when he spoke of how people have become callous and blind…Various people asked him questions, but you were content just to look at his face and could not take your eyes away; you saw a mysterious and wondrous light surrounding him.
>
> Let me tell you something about St. Anthony the Great.[279] Three important visitors came to Anthony: two constantly asked him questions, and Anthony answered. The third asked nothing, but just looked at him in silence. Finally Anthony asked him: "How many times has it been that

you have visited me, and you never ask me a single thing. Why?" The man answered: "Father, for me it is enough just to look at you."

What can I tell you about the light of the righteous? [*Bishop Nikolai notes at the end of the letter.*] This is the light of the spirit which shines through the body, the light of heaven which is directly manifested physically, the foretaste of the light with which the righteous will shine, like the sun, in the Kingdom of Christ.[280]

This silent individual had no questions for St Anthony. It was enough for him to intuitively apprehend the saint's holiness through the ontological receptor, the *nous*.

May people become more aware and trusting of their God-given capability of noetic perception, leading them to reflect the light of Christ in their own small, humble way. As Philip Sherrard so aptly put it: the very "idea that man can be human apart from God is a false idea … The very concept of man implies a relationship, a connection with God." To disregard the heart-centered *nous* and its spiritual capacity makes a person less human, less of what God intended him to be. Conversely, one who strives for the lofty goal of deification is on his way to fully realizing his human potential. Fyodor Dostoevsky, who continues to live on through his books, has shown the power of the *nous* as an ontological receptor within the human heart. Authors of our own time have confirmed its significance. There is even mounting scientific evidence of its existence. May the following words of Ivan Ilyin inspire all hearts who seek God's truth:

We have entered a new age. A time has come for bold faith, a religiosity that is spiritual and pro-active, arising from the heart, being built by reflection from the heart, establishing its own certainty and rationality, knowing its own way, holistically sincere, leading man through humility and sobriety to union with God.[281]

The world will continue to insist that Christians are ridiculous and will laugh at them; they may even be persecuted for their Christian faith. Let them continue undaunted, however, remembering the words of our Lord and Saviour Jesus Christ: "In the world you will have tribulation. But take heart; I have overcome the world" (John 16:33).

ACKNOWLEDGMENTS

I attribute the impetus of this volume to a dedicated group of professors at the Great Books Honors College (Faulkner University, Montgomery, Alabama): Dr Robert Woods, Dr Chad Redwing, Dr David Stark, Dr Michael Young, and Dr Jason Jewell. Their stimulating online group discussions (as part of the Great Conversation) brought together for me the fields of religion, philosophy, literature, and history to form the basis of my Master's thesis and, eventually, this book. Special thanks also go to Dr David Bradshaw, professor of Philosophy at the University of Kentucky, for his cogent advice and resource suggestions.

I stand in awe of the Orthodox Holy Fathers who directly experienced deification and wrote about it for our benefit and instruction. I deeply respect the literary legacy of F.M. Dostoevsky and many other illustrious authors listed in the Bibliography. David Magarshack has done an excellent translation of "The Dream of a Ridiculous Man," which is included in this book with the kind permission of Random House, Inc.

The following individuals helped me tremendously with their meticulous proofreading and suggestions: Mary Mansur, Monk-Subdeacon Theophan (Jensen), and Elena Perekrestov, along with the dedicated staff of Holy Trinity Publications.

Lastly, I would like to thank my husband, Father Gregory Naumenko, and my entire family for their patience and support during the writing of this book. It would not have gone to print without your love and encouragement.

APPENDIX

The Dream of a Ridiculous Man
A Fantastic Story
by F.M. Dostoevsky, translated by David Magershack

I

I am a ridiculous man. They call me a madman now. That would be a distinct rise in my social position were it not that they still regard me as being as ridiculous as ever. But that does not make me angry any more. They are all dear to me now even while they laugh at me—yes, even then they are for some reason particularly dear to me. I shouldn't have minded laughing with them—not at myself, of course, but because I love them—had I not felt so sad as I looked at them. I feel sad because they do not know the truth, whereas I know it. Oh, how hard it is to be the only man to know the truth! But they won't understand that. No, they will not understand.

And yet in the past I used to be terribly distressed at appearing to be ridiculous. No, not appearing to be, but being. I've always cut a ridiculous figure. I suppose I must have known it from the day I was born. At any rate, I've known for certain that I was ridiculous ever since I was seven years old. Afterwards I went to school, then to the university, and—well—the more I learned, the more conscious did I become of the fact that I was ridiculous. So that for me my years of hard work at the university seem in the end to have existed for the sole purpose of demonstrating and proving to me, the more deeply engrossed I became in my studies, that I was an utterly absurd person. And as during my studies, so all my life. Every year the same consciousness that I was ridiculous in every way strengthened and intensified in my mind. They always laughed at me. But not one of them knew or suspected that if there were one man on earth who knew better than anyone else that he was ridiculous, that man was I. And this—I mean, the fact that they did not know it—was the bitterest pill for me to swallow. But there I was myself at fault. I was always so proud that I never wanted to confess it to anyone. No, I wouldn't do that for anything in the world. As the years passed, this pride increased in me so that I do believe that if ever I had by chance confessed it to any one I should have blown my brains out the same evening. Oh, how I suffered in the days of my youth from the thought that I might not myself resist the impulse to confess it to my schoolfellows. But ever since I became a man I grew for some unknown reason a little more composed in my mind, though I was more and more conscious of that awful characteristic of mine. Yes, most decidedly for some unknown reason, for to this day I have not been able to find out why that was so. Perhaps it was because I was becoming terribly disheartened owing to one circumstance which was beyond my power to control, namely, the conviction which was gaining upon me that nothing in the whole world *made any difference.* I had long felt it dawning upon me, but I was fully convinced of it only last year, and that, too, all of a sudden, as it were. I suddenly felt that it made *no* difference to me whether the world existed or whether nothing existed anywhere at all. I began to be acutely conscious that *nothing existed in my own lifetime.* At first I couldn't help feeling that at any rate in the past many things had existed; but later on I came to the conclusion that there had not been anything even in the past, but that for some reason it had merely seemed to have been. Little by little I became convinced that there would be nothing in the future, either. It was then that I suddenly ceased to be angry with people and almost stopped noticing them. This indeed disclosed itself in the smallest trifles. For instance, I would knock against people while walking in the street. And not because I was lost in thought— I had nothing to think about— I had stopped thinking about anything at that time: it made no difference to me. Not that I had found an answer to all the questions. Oh, I had not settled a single question, and there were thousands of them! But *it made no difference to me,* and all the questions disappeared.

And, well, it was only after that that I learnt the truth. I learnt the truth last November, on the third of November, to be precise, and every moment since then has been imprinted indelibly on my mind. It happened on a dismal evening, as dismal an evening as could be imagined. I was returning home at about eleven o'clock and I remember thinking all the time that there could not be a more dismal evening. Even the weather was foul. It had been pouring all day, and the rain too was the coldest and most dismal rain that ever was, a sort of menacing rain— remember that—a rain with a distinct animosity towards people. But about eleven o'clock it had stopped suddenly, and a horrible dampness descended upon everything, and it became much damper and colder than when it had been raining. And a sort of steam was rising from everything, from every cobble in the street, and from every side-street if you peered closely into it from the street as far as the eye could reach. I could not help feeling that if the gaslight had been extinguished everywhere, everything would have seemed much more cheerful, and that the gaslight oppressed the heart so much just because it shed a light upon it all. I had had scarcely any dinner that day. I had been spending the whole evening with an engineer who had two more friends visiting him. I never opened my mouth, and I expect I must have got on their nerves. They were discussing some highly controversial subject, and suddenly got very excited over it. But it really did not make any difference to them. I could see that. I knew that their excitement was not genuine. So I suddenly blurted it out. "My dear fellows," I said, "you don't really care a damn about it, do you?" They were not in the least offended, but they all burst out laughing at me. That was because I had said it without meaning to rebuke them, but simply because it made no difference to me. Well, they realised that it made no difference to me, and they felt happy.

When I was thinking about the gaslight in the streets, I looked up at the sky. The sky was awfully dark, but I could clearly distinguish the torn wisps of cloud and between them fathomless dark patches. All of a sudden I became aware of a little star in one of those patches and I began looking at it intently. That was because the little star gave me an idea: I made up my mind to kill myself that night. I had made up my mind to kill myself already two months before and, poor as I am, I bought myself an excellent revolver and loaded it the same day. But two months had elapsed and it was still lying in the drawer. I was so utterly indifferent to everything that I was anxious to wait for the moment when I would not be so indifferent and then kill myself. Why—I don't know. And so every night during these two months I thought of shooting myself as I was going home. I was only waiting for the right moment. And now the little star gave me an idea, and I made up my mind then and there that it should *most certainly* be that night. But why the little star gave me the idea—I don't know.

And just as I was looking at the sky, this little girl suddenly grasped me by the elbow. The street was already deserted and there was scarcely a soul to be seen. In the distance a cabman was fast asleep on his box. The girl was about eight years old. She had a kerchief on her head, and she wore only an old, shabby little dress. She was soaked to the skin, but what stuck in my memory was her little torn wet boots. I still remember them. They caught my eye especially. She suddenly began tugging at my elbow and calling me. She was not crying, but saying something in a loud, jerky sort of voice, something that did not make sense, for she was trembling all over and her teeth were chattering from cold. She seemed to be terrified of something and she was crying desperately, "Mummy! Mummy!" I turned round to look at her, but did not utter a word and went on walking. But she ran after me and kept tugging at my clothes, and there was a sound in her voice which in very frightened children signifies despair. I know that sound. Though her words sounded as if they were choking her, I realised that her mother must be dying somewhere very near, or that something similar was happening to her, and that she had run out to call someone, to find someone who would help her mother. But I did not go with her; on the contrary, something made me drive her away. At first I told her to go and find a policeman. But she suddenly clasped her hands and, whimpering and gasping for breath, kept running at my side and would not leave me. It was then that I stamped my foot and shouted at her. She just cried, "Sir! Sir! … " and then she left me suddenly and rushed headlong across the road: another man appeared there and she evidently rushed from me to him.

I climbed to the fifth floor. I live apart from my landlord. We all have separate rooms as in an hotel. My room is very small and poor. My window is a semicircular skylight. I have a sofa covered with American cloth, a table with books on it, two chairs and a comfortable armchair, a very old armchair indeed, but low-seated and with a high back serving as a head-rest. I sat down in the armchair, lighted the candle, and began thinking. Next door in the other room behind the partition, the usual bedlam was going on. It had been going on since the day before yesterday. A retired army captain lived there, and he had visitors—six merry gentlemen who drank vodka and played faro with an old pack of cards. Last night they had a fight and I know that two of them were for a long time pulling each other about by the hair. The landlady wanted to complain, but she is dreadfully afraid of the captain. We had only one more lodger in our rooms, a thin little lady, the wife of an army officer, on a visit to Petersburg with her three little children who had all been taken ill since their arrival at our house. She and her children were simply terrified of the captain and they lay shivering and crossing themselves all night long, and the youngest child had a sort of nervous attack from fright. This captain (I know that for a fact) sometimes stops people on Nevsky Avenue and asks them for a few coppers, telling them he is very poor. He can't get a job in the Civil Service, but the strange thing is (and that's why I am telling you this) that the captain had never once during the month he had been living with us made me feel in the least irritated. From the very first, of course, I would not have anything to do with him, and he himself was bored with me the very first time we met. But however big a noise they raised behind their partition and however many of them there were in the captain's room, it makes no difference to me. I sit up all night and, I assure you, I don't hear them at all—so completely do I forget about them. You see, I stay awake all night till daybreak, and that has been going on for a whole year now. I sit up all night in the armchair at the table—doing nothing. I read books only in the daytime. At night I sit like that without even thinking about anything in particular: some thoughts wander in and out of my mind, and I let them come and go as they please. In the night the candle burns out completely.

I sat down at the table, took the gun out of the drawer, and put it down in front of me. I remember asking myself as I put it down, "Is it to be then?" and I replied with complete certainty, "It is!" That is to say, I was going to shoot myself. I knew I should shoot myself that night for certain. What I did not know was how much longer I should go on sitting at the table till I shot myself. And I should of course have shot myself, had it not been for the little girl.

II

You see, though nothing made any difference to me, I could feel pain, for instance, couldn't I? If anyone had struck me, I should have felt pain. The same was true so far as my moral perceptions were concerned. If anything happened to arouse my pity, I should have felt pity, just as I used to do at the time when things did make a difference to me. So I had felt pity that night: I should most decidedly have helped a child. Why then did I not help the little girl? Because of a thought that had occurred to me at the time: when she was pulling at me and calling me, a question suddenly arose in my mind and I could not settle it. It was an idle question, but it made me angry. What made me angry was the conclusion I drew from the reflection that if I had really decided to do away with myself that night, everything in the world should have been more indifferent to me than ever. Why then should I have suddenly felt that I was not indifferent and be sorry for the little girl? I remember that I was very sorry for her, so much so that I felt a strange pang which was quite incomprehensible in my position. I'm afraid I am unable better to convey that fleeting sensation of mine, but it persisted with me at home when I was sitting at the table, and I was very much irritated. I had not been so irritated for a long time past. One train of thought followed another. It was clear to me that so long as I was still a human being and not a meaningless cipher, and till I became a cipher, I was alive, and consequently able to suffer, be angry, and feel shame at my actions. Very well. But if, on the other hand, I were going to kill myself in, say, two hours, what did that little girl matter to me and what did I care for shame or anything else in the world? I was going to turn into a cipher, into an absolute cipher. And surely the realisation that I should soon cease to exist *altogether,* and hence everything would cease to exist, ought to have had some slight effect on my feeling of pity for the little girl or on my feeling of shame after so mean an action. Why after all did I stamp and shout so fiercely at the little girl? I did it because I thought that not only did I feel no pity, but that it wouldn't matter now if I were guilty of the most inhuman baseness, since in another two hours everything would become extinct. Do you believe me when I tell you that that was the only reason why I shouted like that? I am almost convinced of it now. It seemed clear to me that life and the world in some way or other depended on me now. It might almost be said that the world seemed to be created for me alone. If I were to shoot myself, the world would cease to exist— for me at any rate. To say nothing of the possibility that nothing would in fact exist for anyone after me and the whole world would dissolve as soon as my consciousness became extinct, would disappear in a twinkling like a phantom, like some integral part of my consciousness, and vanish without leaving a trace behind, for all this world and all these people exist perhaps only in my consciousness.

I remember that as I sat and meditated, I began to examine all these questions which thronged in my mind one after another from quite a different angle, and thought of something quite new. For instance, the strange notion occurred to me that if I had lived before on the moon or on Mars and had committed there the most shameful and dishonourable action that can be imagined, and had been so disgraced and dishonoured there as can be imagined and experienced only occasionally in a dream, a nightmare, and if, finding myself afterwards on earth, I had retained the memory of what I had done on the other planet, and moreover knew that I should never in any circumstances go back there—if that were to have happened, should I or should I not have felt, as I looked from the earth upon the moon, that *it made no difference* to me? Should I or should I not have felt ashamed of that action? The questions were idle and useless, for the gun was already lying before me and there was not a shadow of doubt in my mind that it was going to take place for certain, but they excited and maddened me. It seemed to me that I could not die now without having settled something first. The little girl, in fact, had saved me, for by these questions I put off my own execution.

Meanwhile things had grown more quiet in the captain's room: they had finished their card game and were getting ready to turn in for the night, and now were only grumbling and swearing at each other in a halfhearted sort of way. It was at that moment that I suddenly fell asleep in my armchair at the table, a thing that had never happened to me before.

I fell asleep without being aware of it at all. Dreams, as we all know, are very curious things: certain incidents in them are presented with quite uncanny vividness, each detail executed with the finishing touch of a jeweller, while others you leap across as though entirely unaware of, for instance, space and time. Dreams seem to be induced not by reason but by desire, not by the head but by the heart, and yet what clever tricks my reason has sometimes played on me in dreams! And furthermore what incomprehensible things happen to it in a dream. My brother, for instance, died five years ago. I sometimes dream about him: he takes a keen interest in my affairs, we are both very interested, and yet I know very well all through my dream that my brother is dead and buried. How is it that I am not surprised that, though dead, he is here beside me, doing his best to help me? Why does my reason accept all this without the slightest hesitation? But enough. Let me tell you about my dream. Yes, I dreamed that dream that night. My dream of the third of November. They are making fun of me now by saying that it was only a dream. But what does it matter whether it was a dream or not, so long as that dream revealed the Truth to me? For once you have recognised the truth and seen it, you know it is the one and only truth and that there can be no other, whether you are asleep or awake. But never mind. Let it be a dream, but remember that I had intended to cut short by suicide the life that means so much to us, and that my dream—my dream—oh, it revealed to me a new, grand, regenerated, strong life!

Listen.

III

I have said that I fell asleep imperceptibly and even while I seemed to be revolving the same thoughts again in my mind. Suddenly I dreamed that I picked up the gun and, sitting in my armchair, pointed it straight at my heart—at my heart, and not at my head. For I had firmly resolved to shoot myself through the head, through the right temple, to be precise. Having aimed the gun at my breast, I paused for a second or two, and suddenly my candle, the table and the wall began moving and swaying before me. I fired quickly.

In a dream you sometimes fall from a great height, or you are being murdered or beaten, but you never feel any pain unless you really manage somehow or other to hurt yourself in bed, when you feel pain and almost always wake up from it. So it was in my dream: I did not feel any pain, but it seemed as though with my shot everything within me was shaken and everything was suddenly extinguished, and a terrible darkness descended all around me. I seemed to have become blind and dumb. I was lying on something hard, stretched out full length on my back. I saw nothing and could not make the slightest movement. All round me people were walking and shouting. The captain was yelling in his deep bass voice, the landlady was screaming and—suddenly another hiatus, and I was being carried in a closed coffin. I could feel the coffin swaying and I was thinking about it, and for the first time the idea flashed through my mind that I was dead, dead as a doornail, that I knew it, that there was not the least doubt about it, that I could neither see nor move, and yet I could feel and reason. But I was soon reconciled to that and, as usually happens in dreams, I accepted the facts without questioning them.

And now I was buried in the earth. They all went away, and I was left alone, entirely alone. I did not move. Whenever before I imagined how I should be buried in a grave, there was only one sensation I actually associated with the grave, namely, that of damp and cold. And so it was now. I felt that I was very cold, especially in the tips of my toes, but I felt nothing else.

I lay in my grave and, strange to say, I did not expect anything, accepting the idea that a dead man had nothing to expect as an incontestable fact. But it was damp. I don't know how long a time passed, whether an hour, or several days, or many days. But suddenly a drop of water, which had seeped through the lid of the coffin, fell on my closed left eye. It was followed by another drop a minute later, then after another minute by another drop, and so on. One drop every minute. All at once deep indignation blazed up in my heart, and I suddenly felt a twinge of physical pain in it. "That's my wound," I thought. "It's the shot I fired. There's a bullet there. …" And drop after drop still kept falling every minute on my closed eyelid. And suddenly I called (not with my voice, for I was motionless, but with the whole of my being) upon Him who was responsible for all that was happening to me:

"Whoever Thou art, and if anything more rational exists than what is happening here, let it, I pray Thee, come to pass here too. But if Thou art revenging Thyself for my senseless act of self-destruction by the infamy and absurdity of life after death, then know that no torture that may be inflicted upon me can ever equal the contempt which I shall go on feeling in silence, though my martyrdom last for aeons upon aeons!"

I made this appeal and was silent. The dead silence went on for almost a minute, and one more drop fell on my closed eyelid, but I knew, I knew and believed infinitely and unshakably that everything would without a doubt change immediately. And then my grave was opened. I don't know, that is, whether it was opened or dug open, but I was seized by some dark and unknown being and we found ourselves in space. I suddenly regained my sight. It was a pitch-black night. Never, never had there been such darkness! We were flying through space at a terrific speed and we had already left the earth behind us. I did not question the being who was carrying me. I was proud and waited. I was telling myself that I was not afraid, and I was filled with admiration at the thought that I was not afraid. I cannot remember how long we were flying, nor can I give you an idea of the time; it all happened as it always does happen in dreams when you leap over space and time and the laws of nature and reason, and only pause at the points which are especially dear to your heart. All I remember is that I suddenly beheld a little star in the darkness.

"Is that Sirius?" I asked, feeling suddenly unable to restrain myself, for I had made up my mind not to ask any questions.

"No," answered the being who was carrying me, "that is the same star you saw between the clouds when you were coming home."

I knew that its face bore some resemblance to a human face. It is a strange fact but I did not like that being, and I even felt an intense aversion for it. I had expected complete non-existence and that was why I had shot myself through the heart. And yet there I was in the hands of a being, not human of course, but which *was,* which existed. "So there is life beyond the grave!" I thought with the curious irrelevance of a dream, but at heart I remained essentially unchanged. "If I must *be* again," I thought, "and live again at someone's unalterable behest, I won't be defeated and humiliated!"

"You know I'm afraid of you and that's why you despise me," I said suddenly to my companion, unable to refrain from the humiliating remark with its implied admission, and feeling my own humiliation in my heart like the sharp prick of a needle.

He did not answer me, but I suddenly felt that I was not despised, that no one was laughing at me, that no one was even pitying me, and that our journey had a purpose, an unknown and mysterious purpose that concerned only me. Fear was steadily growing in my heart. Something was communicated to me from my silent companion—mutely but agonisingly—and it seemed to permeate my whole being. We were speeding through dark and unknown regions of space. I had long since lost sight of the constellations familiar to me. I knew that there were stars in the heavenly spaces whose light took thousands and millions of years to reach the earth. Possibly we were already flying through those spaces. I expected something in the terrible anguish that wrung my heart. And suddenly a strangely familiar and incredibly nostalgic feeling shook me to the very core: I suddenly caught sight of our sun! I knew that it could not possibly be *our* sun that gave birth to our earth, and that we were millions of miles away from our sun, but for some unknown reason I recognised with every fibre of my being that it was precisely the same sun as ours, its exact copy and twin. A sweet, nostalgic feeling filled my heart with rapture: the old familiar power of the same light which had given me life stirred an echo in my heart and revived it, and I felt the same life stirring within me for the first time since I had been in the grave.

"But if it is the sun, if it's exactly the same sun as ours," I cried, "then where is the earth?"

And my companion pointed to a little star twinkling in the darkness with an emerald light. We were making straight for it.

"But are such repetitions possible in the universe? Can that be nature's law? And if that is an earth there, is it the same earth as ours? Just the same poor, unhappy, but dear, dear earth, and beloved for ever and ever? Arousing like our earth the same poignant love for herself even in the most ungrateful of her children?" I kept crying, deeply moved by an uncontrollable, rapturous love for the dear old earth I had left behind.

The face of the poor little girl I had treated so badly flashed through my mind.

"You shall see it all," answered my companion, and a strange sadness sounded in his voice.

But we were rapidly approaching the planet. It was growing before my eyes. I could already distinguish the ocean, the outlines of Europe, and suddenly a strange feeling of some great and sacred jealousy blazed up in my heart.

"How is such a repetition possible and why? I love, I can only love the earth I've left behind, stained with my blood when, ungrateful wretch that I am, I extinguished my life by shooting myself through the heart.

But never, never have I ceased to love that earth, and even on the night I parted from it I loved it perhaps more poignantly than ever. Is there suffering on this new earth? On our earth we can truly love only with suffering and through suffering! We know not how to love otherwise. We know no other love. I want suffering in order to love. I want and thirst this very minute to kiss, with tears streaming down my cheeks, the one and only earth I have left behind. I don't want, I won't accept life on any other!…"

But my companion had already left me. Suddenly, and without as it were being aware of it myself, I stood on this other earth in the bright light of a sunny day, fair and beautiful as paradise. I believe I was standing on one of the islands which on our earth form the Greek archipelago, or somewhere on the coast of the mainland close to this archipelago. Oh, everything was just as it is with us, except that everything seemed to be bathed in the radiance of some public festival and of some great and holy triumph attained at last. The gentle emerald sea softly lapped the shore and kissed it with manifest, visible, almost conscious love. Tall, beautiful trees stood in all the glory of their green luxuriant foliage, and their innumerable leaves (I am sure of that) welcomed me with their soft, tender rustle, and seemed to utter sweet words of love. The lush grass blazed with bright and fragrant flowers. Birds were flying in flocks through the air and, without being afraid of me, alighted on my shoulders and hands and joyfully beat against me with their sweet fluttering wings. And at last I saw and came to know the people of this blessed earth. They came to me themselves. They surrounded me. They kissed me. Children of the sun, children of their sun—oh, how beautiful they were! Never on our earth had I beheld such beauty in man. Only perhaps in our children during the very first years of their life could one have found a remote, though faint, reflection of this beauty. The eyes of these happy people shone with a bright lustre. Their faces were radiant with understanding and a serenity of mind that had reached its greatest fulfilment. Those faces were joyous; in the words and voices of these people there was a child-like gladness. Oh, at the first glance at their faces I at once understood all, all! It was an earth unstained by the Fall, inhabited by people who had not sinned and who lived in the same paradise as that in which, according to the legends of mankind, our first parents lived before they sinned, with the only difference that all the earth here was everywhere the same paradise. These people, laughing happily, thronged round me and overwhelmed me with their caresses; they took me home with them, and each of them was anxious to set my mind at peace. Oh, they asked me no questions, but seemed to know everything already (that was the impression I got), and they longed to remove every trace of suffering from my face as soon as possible.

IV

Well, you see, again let me repeat: All right, let us assume it was only a dream! But the sensation of the love of those innocent and beautiful people has remained with me forever, and I can feel that their love is even now flowing out to me from over there. I have seen them myself. I have known them thoroughly and been convinced. I loved them and I suffered for them afterwards. Oh, I knew at once even all the time that there were many things about them I should never be able to understand. To me, a modern Russian progressive and a despicable citizen of Petersburg, it seemed inexplicable that, knowing so much, they knew nothing of our science, for instance. But I soon realised that their knowledge was derived from, and fostered by emotions other than those to which we were accustomed on earth, and that their aspirations, too, were quite different. They desired nothing. They were at peace with themselves. They did not strive to gain knowledge of life as we strive to understand it because their lives were full. But their knowledge was higher and deeper than the knowledge we derive from our science; for our science seeks to explain what life is and strives to understand it in order to teach others how to live, while they knew how to live without science. I understood that, but I couldn't understand their knowledge. They pointed out their trees to me and I could not understand the intense love with which they looked on them; it was as though they were talking with beings like themselves. And, you know, I don't think I am exaggerating in saying that they talked with them! Yes, they had discovered their language, and I am sure the trees understood them. They looked upon all nature like that—the animals which lived peaceably with them and did not attack them, but loved them, conquered by their love for them. They pointed out the stars to me and talked to me about them in a way that I could not understand, but I am certain that in some curious way they communed with the stars in the heavens, not only in thought, but in some actual, living way. Oh, these people were not concerned whether I understood them or not; they loved me without it. But I too knew that they would never be able to understand me, and for that reason I hardly ever spoke to them about our earth. I merely kissed the earth on which they lived in their presence, and worshipped them without any words. And they saw that and let me worship them without being ashamed that I was worshipping them, for they themselves loved much. They did not suffer for me when, weeping, I sometimes kissed their feet, for in their hearts they were joyfully aware of the strong affection with which they would return my love. At times I asked myself in amazement how they had managed never to offend a person like me and not once arouse in a person like me a feeling of jealousy and envy. Many times I asked myself how I—a braggart and a liar—could refrain from telling them all I knew of science and philosophy, of which of course they had no idea? How it had never occurred to me to impress them with my store of learning, or impart my learning to them out of the love I bore them?

They were playful and high-spirited like children. They wandered about their beautiful woods and groves, they sang their beautiful songs, they lived on simple food—the fruits of their trees, the honey from their woods, and the milk of the animals that loved them. To obtain their food and clothes, they did not work very hard or long. They knew love and they begot children, but I never noticed in them those outbursts of *cruel* sensuality which overtake almost everybody on our earth, whether man or woman, and are the only source of almost every sin of our human race. They rejoiced in their new-born children as new sharers in their bliss. There were no quarrels or jealousy among them, and they did not even know what the words meant. Their children were the children of them all, for they were all one family. There was scarcely any illness among them, though there was death; but their old people died peacefully, as though falling asleep, surrounded by the people who took leave of them, blessing them and smiling at them, and themselves receiving with bright smiles the farewell wishes of their friends. I never saw grief or tears on those occasions. What I did see was love that seemed to reach the point of rapture, but it was a gentle, self-sufficient, and contemplative rapture. There was reason to believe that they communicated with the departed after death, and that their earthly union was not cut short by death. They found it almost impossible to understand me when I questioned them about life eternal, but apparently they were so convinced of it in their minds that for them it was no question at all. They had no places of worship, but they had a certain awareness of a constant, uninterrupted, and living union with the Universe at large. They had no specific religions, but instead they had a certain knowledge that when their earthly joy had reached the limits imposed upon it by nature, they— both the living and the dead—would reach a state of still closer communion with the Universe at large. They looked forward to that moment with joy, but without haste and without pining for it, as though already possessing it in the vague stirrings of their hearts, which they communicated to each other.

In the evening, before going to sleep, they were fond of gathering together and singing in melodious and harmonious choirs. In their songs they expressed all the sensations the parting day had given them. They praised it and bade it farewell. They praised nature, the earth, the sea, and the woods. They were also fond of composing songs about one another, and they praised each other like children. Their songs were very simple, but they sprang straight from the heart and they touched the heart. And not only in their songs alone, but they seemed to spend all their lives in perpetual praise of one another. It seemed to be a universal and all-embracing love for each other. Some of their songs were solemn and ecstatic, and I was scarcely able to understand them at all. While understanding the words, I could never entirely fathom their meaning. It remained somehow beyond the grasp of my reason, and yet it sank unconsciously deeper and deeper into my heart. I often told them that I had had a presentiment of it years ago and that all that joy and glory had been perceived by me while I was still on our earth as a nostalgic yearning, bordering at times on unendurably poignant sorrow; that I had had a presentiment of them all and of their glory in the dreams of my heart and in the reveries of my soul; that often on our earth I could not look at the setting sun without tears. … That there always was a sharp pang of anguish in my hatred of the men of our earth; why could I not hate them without loving them too? why could I not forgive them? And in my love for them, too, there was a sharp pang of anguish: why could I not love them without hating them? They listened to me, and I could tell that they did not know what I was talking about. But I was not sorry to have spoken to them of it, for I knew that they appreciated how much and how anxiously I yearned for those I had forsaken. Oh yes, when they looked at me with their dear eyes full of love, when I realised that in their presence my heart, too, became as innocent and truthful as theirs, I did not regret my inability to understand them, either. The sensation of the fullness of life left me breathless, and I worshipped them in silence.

Oh, everyone laughs in my face now and everyone assures me that I could not possibly have seen and felt anything so definite, but was merely conscious of a sensation that arose in my own feverish heart, and that I invented all those details myself when I woke up. And when I told them that they were probably right, good Lord, what mirth that admission of mine caused and how they laughed at me! Why, of course, I was overpowered by the mere sensation of that dream and it alone survived in my sorely wounded heart. But none the less the real shapes and forms of my dream, that is, those I actually saw at the very time of my dream, were filled with such harmony and were so enchanting and beautiful, and so intensely true, that on awakening I was indeed unable to clothe them in our feeble words so that they were bound as it were to become blurred in my mind; so is it any wonder that perhaps unconsciously I was myself afterwards driven to make up the details which I could not help distorting, particularly in view of my passionate desire to convey some of them at least as quickly as I could. But that does not mean that I have no right to believe that it all did happen. As a matter of fact, it was quite possibly a thousand times better, brighter, and more joyful than I describe it. What if it was only a dream? All that couldn't possibly not have been. And do you know, I think I'll tell you a secret: perhaps it was no dream at all! For what happened afterwards was so awful, so horribly true, that it couldn't possibly have been a mere coinage of my brain seen in a dream. Granted that my heart was responsible for my dream, but could my heart alone have been responsible for the awful truth of what happened to me afterwards? Surely my paltry heart and my vacillating and trivial mind could not have risen to such a revelation of truth! Oh, judge for yourselves: I have been concealing it all the time, but now I will tell you the whole truth. The fact is, I—corrupted them all!

V

Yes, yes, it ended in my corrupting them all! How it could have happened I do not know, but I remember it clearly. The dream encompassed thousands of years and left in me only a vague sensation of the whole. I only know that the cause of the Fall was I. Like a horrible trichina, like the germ of the plague infecting whole kingdoms, so did I infect with myself all that happy earth that knew no sin before me. They learnt to lie, and they grew to appreciate the beauty of a lie. Oh, perhaps, it all began *innocently,* with a jest, with a desire to show off, with amorous play, and perhaps indeed only with a germ, but this germ made its way into their hearts and they liked it. The voluptuousness was soon born, voluptuousness begot jealousy, and jealousy—cruelty … . Oh, I don't know, I can't remember, but soon, very soon the first blood was shed; they were shocked and horrified, and they began to separate and to shun one another. They formed alliances, but it was one against another. Recriminations began, reproaches. They came to know shame, and they made shame into a virtue. The conception of honour was born, and every alliance raised its own standard. They began torturing animals, and the animals ran away from them into the forests and became their enemies. A struggle began for separation, for isolation, for personality, for mine and thine. They began talking in different languages. They came to know sorrow, and they loved sorrow. They thirsted for suffering, and they said that Truth could only be attained through suffering. It was then that science made its appearance among them. When they became wicked, they began talking of brotherhood and humanity and understood the meaning of those ideas. When they became guilty of crimes, they invented justice, and drew up whole codes of law, and to ensure the carrying out of their laws they erected a guillotine. They only vaguely remembered what they had lost, and they would not believe that they ever were happy and innocent. They even laughed at the possibility of their former happiness and called it a dream. They could not even imagine it in any definite shape or form, but the strange and wonderful thing was that though they had lost faith in their former state of happiness and called it a fairy-tale, they longed so much to be happy and innocent once more that, like children, they succumbed to the desire of their hearts, glorified this desire, built temples, and began offering up prayers to their own idea, their own "desire," and at the same time firmly believed that it could not be realised and brought about, though they still worshipped it and adored it with tears. And yet if they could have in one way or another returned to the state of happy innocence they had lost, and if someone had shown it to them again and had asked them whether they desired to go back to it, they would certainly have refused. The answer they gave me was, "What if we are dishonest, cruel, and unjust? We *know* it and we are sorry for it, and we torment ourselves for it, and inflict pain upon ourselves, and punish ourselves more perhaps than the merciful Judge who will judge us and whose name we do not know. But we have science and with its aid we shall again discover truth, though we shall accept it only when we perceive it with our reason. Knowledge is higher than feeling, and the consciousness of life is higher than life. Science will give us wisdom. Wisdom will reveal to us the laws. And the knowledge of the laws of happiness is higher than happiness." That is what they said to me, and having uttered those words, each of them began to love himself better than anyone else, and

indeed they could not do otherwise. Every one of them became so jeal-
ous of his own personality that he strove with might and main to belit-
tle and humble it in others; and therein he saw the whole purpose of
his life. Slavery made its appearance, even voluntary slavery: the weak
eagerly submitted themselves to the will of the strong on condition that
the strong helped them to oppress those who were weaker than themselves. Saints made their appearance, saints who came to these people
with tears and told them of their pride, of their loss of proportion and
harmony, of their loss of shame. They were laughed to scorn and stoned
to death. Their sacred blood was spilt on the threshold of the temples.
But then men arose who began to wonder how they could all be united
again, so that everybody should, without ceasing to love himself best
of all, not interfere with everybody else and so that all of them should
live together in a society which would at least seem to be founded on
mutual understanding. Whole wars were fought over this idea. All the
combatants at one and the same time firmly believed that science, wisdom, and the instinct of self-preservation would in the end force mankind to unite into a harmonious and intelligent society, and therefore,
to hasten matters, the "very wise" did their best to exterminate as rapidly as possible the "not so wise" who did not understand their idea, so
as to prevent them from interfering with its triumph. But the instinct
of self-preservation began to weaken rapidly. Proud and voluptuous
men appeared who frankly demanded all or nothing. In order to obtain
everything they did not hesitate to resort to violence, and if it failed—to
suicide. Religions were founded to propagate the cult of non-existence
and self-destruction for the sake of the everlasting peace in nothingness.
At last these people grew weary of their senseless labours and suffering appeared on their faces, and these people proclaimed that suffering
was beauty, for in suffering alone was there thought. They glorified suffering in their songs. I walked among them, wringing my hands and
weeping over them, but I loved them perhaps more than before when
there was no sign of suffering in their faces and when they were innocent and—oh, so beautiful! I loved the earth they had polluted even
more than when it had been a paradise, and only because sorrow had

made its appearance on it. Alas, I always loved sorrow and affliction, but only for myself, only for myself; for them I wept now, for I pitied them. I stretched out my hands to them, accusing, cursing, and despising myself. I told them that I alone was responsible for it all—I alone; that it was I who had brought them corruption, contamination, and lies! I implored them to crucify me, and I taught them how to make the cross. I could not kill myself; I had not the courage to do it; but I longed to receive martyrdom at their hands. I thirsted for martyrdom, I yearned for my blood to be shed to the last drop in torment and suffering. But they only laughed at me, and in the end they began looking upon me as a madman. They justified me. They said that they had got what they themselves wanted and that what was now could not have been otherwise. At last they told me that I was becoming dangerous to them and that they would lock me up in a lunatic asylum if I did not hold my peace. Then sorrow entered my soul with such force that my heart was wrung and I felt as though I were dying, and then—well, then I awoke.

It was morning, that is, the sun had not risen yet, but it was about six o'clock. When I came to, I found myself in the same armchair, my candle had burnt out, in the captain's room they were asleep, and silence, so rare in our house, reigned around. The first thing I did was to jump up in great amazement. Nothing like this had ever happened to me before, not even so far as the most trivial details were concerned. Never, for instance, had I fallen asleep like this in my armchair. Then, suddenly, as I was standing and coming to myself, I caught sight of my gun lying there ready and loaded. But I pushed it away from me at once! Oh, how I longed for life, life! I lifted up my hands and called upon eternal Truth—no, not called upon it, but wept. Rapture, infinite and boundless rapture intoxicated me. Yes, life and—preaching! I made up my mind to preach from that very moment and, of course, to go on preaching all my life. I am going to preach, I want to preach. What? Why, truth. For I have beheld truth, I have beheld it with mine own eyes, I have beheld it in all its glory!

And since then I have been preaching. Moreover, I love all who laugh at me more than all the rest. Why that is so, I don't know and I cannot explain, but let it be so. They say that even now I often get muddled and confused and that if I am getting muddled and confused now, what will be later on? It is perfectly true. I do get muddled and confused and it is quite possible that I shall be getting worse later. And, of course, I shall get muddled several times before I find out how to preach, that is, what words to use and what deeds to perform, for that is all very difficult! All this is even now as clear to me as daylight, but, pray, tell me who does not get muddled and confused? And yet all follow the same path, at least all strive to achieve the same thing, from the philosopher to the lowest criminal, only by different roads. It is an old truth, but this is what is new: I cannot even get very much muddled and confused. For I have beheld the Truth. I have beheld it and I know that people can be happy and beautiful without losing their ability to live on earth. I will not and I cannot believe that evil is the normal condition among men. And yet they all laugh at this faith of mine. But how can I help believing it? I have beheld it—the Truth—it is not as though I had invented it with my mind: I have beheld it, I have beheld it, and the *living image* of it has filled my soul forever. I have beheld it in all its glory and I cannot believe that it cannot exist among men. So how can I grow muddled and confused? I shall of course lose my way and I'm afraid that now and again I may speak with words that are not my own, but not for long: the living image of what I beheld will always be with me and it will always correct me and lead me back on to the right path. Oh, I'm in fine fettle, and I am of good cheer. I will go on and on for a thousand years, if need be. Do you know, at first I did not mean to tell you that I corrupted them, but that was a mistake—there you have my first mistake! But Truth whispered to me that I was *lying,* and so preserved me and set me on the right path. But I'm afraid I do not know how to establish a heaven on earth, for I do not know how to put it into words. After my dream I lost the knack of putting things into words. At least, into the most necessary and most important words. But never mind, I shall go on and I shall keep on talking, for I have indeed beheld it with my own eyes, though I cannot describe what I saw. It is this the scoffers do not understand. "He had a dream," they say, "a vision, a hallucination!" Oh dear, is this all they have to say? Do they really think that is very clever? And how proud they are! A dream! What is a dream? And what about our life? Is that not a dream too? I will say more: even—yes, even if this never comes to pass, even if there never is a heaven on earth (that, at any rate, I can see very well!), even then I shall go on preaching. And really how simple it all is: in one day, *in one hour,* everything could be arranged at once! The main thing is to love your neighbour as yourself—that is the main thing, and that is everything, for nothing else matters. Once you do that, you will discover at once how everything can be arranged. And yet it is an old truth, a truth that has been told over and over again, but in spite of that it finds no place among men! "The consciousness of life is higher than life, the knowledge of happiness is higher than happiness"—that is what we have to fight against! And I shall, I shall fight against it! If only we all wanted it, everything could be arranged immediately.

And—I did find that little girl. ... And I shall go on! I shall go on!

BIBLIOGRAPHY

Ackrill, J. L. *Aristotle the Philosopher*. New York: Oxford University Press, 1990.

Adler, Mortimer J. *The Great Conversation*. Great Books of the Western World, Vol. 1. Chicago: Encyclopedia Britannica, 1986.

Adler, Mortimer J. *Introduction and Syntopical Guide*, Gateway to the Great Books, Chapter 5, Philosophy. Chicago, Illinois: Encyclopedia Britannica, Inc. William Benton, Publisher, 1963. Online source: https://archive.org/details/in.ernet.dli.2015.460705/page/n101

Annas, Julia. *Ancient Philosophy: A Very Short Introduction*. New York: Oxford University Press, 2000.

Aquinas, Thomas. *Contra Errores Graecorum*. Translated by Peter Damian Fehlman. Accessed June 10, 2014. http://dhspriory.org/thomas/ContraErr-Graecorum.htm

Aristotle. *Metaphysics*. Translated by Richard Hope. Ann Arbor: University of Michigan Press, 2007.

St Athanasius of Alexandria. *On the Incarnation*. Crestwood, NY: St. Vladimir's Seminary Press, 1996.

St Augustine, Bishop of Hippo. *City of God*. *Nicene and Post-Nicene Fathers*. Vol. 2. Edited by Philip Schaff. Peabody, MA: Hendrickson Publishers, 1995.

St Augustine, Bishop of Hippo. *On Christian Teaching*. Translated by J. F. Shaw. Overland, Kansas: Digireads.com Publishing, 2009.

Bloom, Allan, trans. *The Republic of Plato*, 2nd Edition, Basic Books. Philadelphia, PA: HarperCollins Publishers, 1991.

Bradshaw, David. *Aristotle East and West*. Cambridge, UK: Cambridge University Press, 2007.

Bradshaw, David. "The Divine Energies in the New Testament." *St. Vladimir's Theological Quarterly* 50, no. 3 (2006): 189–223.

Bradshaw, David. "The Mind and the Heart in the Christian East and West." *Faith and Philosophy* 26, no. 5 (2009): 576–598.

St Clement of Alexandria. *The Stromata*. *The Ante-Nicene Fathers*. Vol. 2. Rev. Alexander Roberts and James Donaldson. Grand Rapids, MI: Wm. B. Erdmann's Publishing Company, 1956.

Christian Classics Ethereal Library. *Fyodor Dostoevsky, Russian Novelist*. Accessed September 28, 2014. http://www.ccel.org/ccel/dostoevsky.

Copleston, Frederick, S. J. *A History of Philosophy, Vol. 1: Greece and Rome, From the Socratics to Plotinus*. New York: An Image Book, Doubleday, 1993.

Davidson, Herbert. *Alfarabi, Avicenna, and Averroes, on Intellect*. Oxford: University Press, 1992.

Dostoevsky, Anna. *Dostoevsky: Reminiscences*. Translated by Beatrice Stillman. New York: Liveright Publishing Corp., 1971.

Dostoevsky, Fyodor. *The Brothers Karamazov*. Translated by Richard Pevear and Larissa Volokhonsky. New York: Farrar, Straus and Giroux, 1990.

Dostoevsky, Fyodor. *Demons*. Translated by Richard Pevear and Larissa Volokhonsky. New York: VintageBooks, A Division of Random House, 1995.

Dostoevsky, Fyodor. "The Dream of a Ridiculous Man." In *The Best Short Stories of Fyodor Dostoevsky*, translated by David Magarshack. New York: The Modern Library, 2001.

Dostoevsky, Fyodor. "The Dream of a Ridiculous Man." Accessed June 16, 2014. http://fiction.eserver.org/short/dream_of_a_ridiculous_man.html

Dostoevsky, Fyodor. *The Idiot*. Translated by Richard Pevear and Larissa Volokhonsky. New York: Vintage Books, A Division of Random House, 2001.

Frank, Joseph. *Dostoevsky: A Writer in His Time*. Princeton, NJ: Princeton University Press, 2010.

Gama, Michael Paul. *Theosis: Patristic Remedy for Evangelical Yearning at the Close of the Modern Age*. Eugene, OR: Wipf & Stock, 2017.

Gamble, Richard M., ed. *The Great Tradition*. Wilmington, DE: ISI Books, 2010.

Heidegger, Martin. *Introduction to Metaphysics*. Translated by Gregory Fried and Richard Polt. New Haven, CT: Yale University Press, 2000.

Hierotheos, Metropolitan of Nafpaktos. *The Mind of the Orthodox Church*. Levadia, Greece: Birth of the Theotokos Monastery, 1998.

Hierotheos, Metropolitan of Nafpaktos. *Orthodox Psychotherapy, the Science of the Fathers*. Translated by Esther Williams. Levadia, Greece: Birth of the Theotokos Monastery, 2006.

Hierotheos, Metropolitan of Nafpaktos. *Saint Gregory Palamas as a Hagiorite*. Levadia, Greece: Birth of the Theotokos Monastery, 2000.

Homer. *The Iliad*. Translated by Robert Fagles. New York: Viking Penguin, 1990.

Hope, Richard, trans. *Aristotle-Metaphysics*. New York: Columbia University Press, 2007.

Ilyin, Ivan. *Axioms of Religious Experience*. Chapter 1, "On the Subjectivity of Religious Experience." Translated by G. E. Henderson. M. Div paper. South Canaan, PA: St. Tikhon's Theological Seminary, 2009.

Ilyin, Ivan. *Аксиомы религиозного опыта* [*Axioms of Religious Experience*]. Moscow: Too Rarog, 1993.

St Irenaeus of Lyons. *Against Heresies, The Ante-Nicene Fathers*. Vol. 1. Translated by Rev. Roberts. Grand Rapids, MI: Eerdmans Printing Company, 1987.

Jensen, Chris. "Shine as the Sun: C.S. Lewis and the Doctrine of Deification." *Pursuit of Truth: A Journal of Christian Scholarship*, October 2007. Accessed October 1, 2014. http://www.cslewis.org/journal/shine-as-the-sun-cs-lewis-and-the-doctrine-of-deification/

St John of Damascus. *An Exact Exposition of the Orthodox Faith*, Book II Chapter 12, 236. Accessed July 4, 2018. https://archive.org/details/AnExactExpositionOfTheOrthodoxFaith.

Kiefer, James E. "Biographical Sketches of Memorable Christians of the Past." *Justin Martyr: Philosopher, Apologist and Martyr*. Accessed June 10, 2014. http://justus.anglican.org/resources/bio/175.html.

Kreeft, Peter, ed. Thomas Aquinas' *Summa of the Summa*. San Francisco: Ignatius Press, 1990.

Lewis, Clive Staples. *Mere Christianity*. San Francisco: HarperCollins Publishers, 1980.

Literature Resource Center. *Fyodor M. Dostoevsky*. Accessed July 14, 2014. http://people.brandeis.edu/~teuber/dostoevskybio.html#BiographicalInfoEssay.

Lossky, Vladimir. *The Mystical Theology of the Eastern Church*. Cambridge: James Clarke & C., 2005.

Lukacs, John. *Historical Consciousness: The Remembered Past*. New Brunswick: Transaction Publishers, 1997.

Lynch, William F. *Christ and Apollo: The Dimensions of the Literary Imagination*. Wilmington, DE: ISI Books, 2003.

Mathewes-Green, Frederica. *Welcome to the Orthodox Church: An Introduction to Eastern Christianity*. Brewster, MA: Paraclete Press, 2015.

St Maximus the Confessor. *On the Cosmic Mystery of Jesus Christ, Ad Thalassium 60*. Crestwood, NJ: St. Vladimir's Press, 2003.

St Maximus the Confessor. *Selected Writings*. Translated by George C. Berthold. New York: Paulist Press, 1985.

McInerny, Ralph. *St. Thomas Aquinas*. Boston, MA: G.K. Hall & Co., 1977.

Mochulsky, Konstantin. *Dostoevsky: His Life and Work*. Translated by Michael A. Minihan. Princeton, NJ: Princeton University Press, 1971.

Palamas, St Gregory. *The Triads*. Mahwah, NJ: Paulist Press, 1983.

Pennock, Dee. *Path to Sanity: Lessons from Ancient Holy Counselors on How to Have a Sound Mind*. Minneapolis, MN: Light and Life Publishing Company, 2010.

Peterson, Jordan B. *12 Rules for Life; An Antidote to Chaos*. Toronto: Random House Canada, 2018.

Pieper, Josef. *Leisure: The Basis of Culture*. San Francisco: Ignatius Press, 2009.

Plato. *Euthyphro. Apology. Crito. Phaedo. Phaedrus*. Cambridge, MA: Harvard University Press, 1999.

Plato. *Republic. Great Books of the Western World*. Vol. 7. Edited by Adler and Hutchins. Chicago: Encyclopedia Britannica, 1952.

Plato. *Republic*. The University of Adelaide Library, Electronic Texts Collection, submitted by Steven Thomas, 1997. Accessed July 14, 2014. http://www.faculty.umb.edu/gary_zabel/Courses/Phil%20281b/Philosophy%20of%20Magic/Phil%20100/Readings/Plato%27s%20Republic.htm.

Plotinus. *First Ennead, Great Books of the Western World*. Vol. 17. Edited by Adler and Hutchins. Chicago: Encyclopedia Britannica, 1952.

Pomazansky, Ioanna. "What Is the Heart?" *Orthodox Life*, no. 6 (November–December 2011): 24–34.

Popovich, Archimandrite Justin. *Философия и религия Ф. М. Достоевского [The Philosophy and Religion of F. M. Dostoevsky]*. Minsk: D. V. Harchenko, 2008.

Rose, Father Seraphim. *The Place of Blessed Augustine in the Orthodox Church*. Platina, CA: St. Herman of Alaska Brotherhood, 1996.

Rossi, Albert S. *Becoming a Healing Presence*. Chesterton, IN: Ancient Faith Publishing, 2014.

Sherrard, Philip. *The Greek East and Latin West*. Limni, Evia, Greece: Denise Harvey, Publisher, 1959.

Sherrard, Philip. *The Rape of Man and Nature, An Enquiry into the Origins and Consequences of Modern Science*. Limni, Evia, Greece: Denise Harvey, Publisher, 1991.

Snell, Bruno. *The Discovery of the Mind in Greek Philosophy and Literature*. "Homer's View of Man." Mineola, NY: Courier Dover Publications, 1960.

Sullivan, Shirley Darcus. *Sophocles' Use of Psychological Terminology: Old and New*. Chapter 4: "Nous in the Tragedies." Toronto: Carleton University Press, 1999.

St Symeon the New Theologian. *The First-Created Man*, Homily 37.4. Translated by Father Seraphim Rose. Platina, CA: St Herman of Alaska Brotherhood, 2013.

St Theophan the Recluse. *Thoughts for Each Day of the Year* (Thursday of the Second Week of Lent). Translated by Lisa Marie Baranov. Platina, CA: St. Herman of Alaska Brotherhood, 2012.

Tatakis, B. N. *Christian Philosophy in the Patristic and Byzantine Tradition*. Rollinsford, NH: Orthodox Research Institute, 2007.

Velimirovich, Bishop Nikolai. *Missionary Letters*. Translated by Hieromonk Serafim Baltic. Grayslake, IL: Joe Buley Memorial Library/New Gracanica Monastery, 2011.

Velimirovich, Bishop Nikolai. *Prologue from Ochrid*. Red Bank, NJ: St. Sergius Publishing House, 1985.

Vorobiev, Abbot Nikon. *Letters to Spiritual Children*. Richfield Springs, NY: Nikodemos Orthodox Publication Society, 2015.

Voyno-Yasenetsky, Archbishop Luke. *Дух, душа и тело* [*Spirit, Soul and Body*]. Edited by N. G. Kutsayeva. Minsk: Byelorussian Publishing House, 2013.

Ware, Timothy (Bishop Kallistos). *The Orthodox Church*. Harmondsworth, Middlesex, England: Penguin Books, 1964.

NOTES

Introduction

1. Shirley Darcus Sullivan, "Nous in the Tragedies," in *Sophocles' Use of Psychological Terminology: Old and New* (Toronto, Canada: Carleton University Press, 1999), 61.
2. Frederick S. J. Copleston, *A History of Philosophy, vol. 1: Greece and Rome, From the Socratics to Plotinus* (New York: An Image Book, Doubleday, 1993), 69.
3. Stanford Encyclopedia of Philosophy, *Anaxagoras*, accessed August 7, 2014, http://plato.stanford.edu/entries/anaxagoras/.
4. St John of Damascus, *An Exact Exposition of the Orthodox Faith*, Book II, Chapter 12, p. 236, accessed July 4, 2018, https://archive.org/details/AnExactExpositionOfTheOrthodoxFaith.
5. St Gregory Palamas, *The Triads* (Mahwah, NJ: Paulist Press, 1983), 118, note 3. Here is the full quote by Fr John Meyendorff: "In patristic usage, these two modes of cognition (mystical and intellectual) correspond to two different human cognitive faculties: the *nous*, the spiritual mind or intuitive intellect, capable of direct apprehension of the truth of things; and the *dianoia*, the analytical and discursive intellect that works out problems by logical stages and knows *about* things."
6. Philip Sherrard, *The Rape of Man and Nature, An Enquiry into the Origins and Consequences of Modern Science* (Limni, Evia, Greece: Denise Harvey, Publisher, 2015), 28.
7. John Lukacs, *Historical Consciousness: The Remembered Past* (New Brunswick: Transaction Publishers, 1997), 5.
8. Ivan Alexandrovich Ilyin (1883–1954), Russian religious and political philosopher.
9. Ivan Ilyin, Аксиомы религиозного опыта [Axioms of Religious Experience] (Moscow: Too Rarog, 1993), 303 (Translated and abbreviated from the Russian—MN).
10. Ibid., 296.

11. The term *theosis*, or deification, is often associated with the quote by St
     Athanasius of Alexandria (299–373 AD) (*On the Incarnation*, 54) that Christ
     "was made man in order that we might be made God." St Athanasius of
     Alexandria, *On the Incarnation*, 54:3, trans. Fr John Behr (Crestwood, NY:
     St Vladimir's Seminary Press, 2012), 107. He is only one of many early Holy
     Fathers who wrote on this subject. For a further explanation of *theosis*,
     see David Bradshaw's *Aristotle East and West* (Cambridge: Cambridge
     University Press, 2007), 173–175.
12. Protagonist: the leading character in a novel or other fictional text.
13. Nihilistic: rejecting all religious and moral principles in the belief that life
     is meaningless.
14. Metropolitan Hierotheos of Nafpaktos, *Orthodox Psychotherapy, the Science
     of the Fathers*, trans. Esther Williams (Levadia, Greece: Birth of the
     Theotokos Monastery, 2006), 164.
15. Metropolitan Hierotheos of Nafpaktos, *Saint Gregory Palamas as a
     Hagiorite* (Levadia, Greece: Birth of the Theotokos Monastery, 2000), 76.
     Although Saint Gregory lived in the fourteenth century, he upheld the
     teaching of the early Church fathers on deification.
16. Hierotheos, *Orthodox Psychotherapy*, 136.
17. Bishop Ignatius Brianchaninov, *The Arena*, trans. Archimandrite Lazarus
     (Jordanville, NY: Holy Trinity Monastery, 2012), 182.
18. Ibid., 213.
19. For example, among the Greek deities is Morpheus, the god of dreams.
20. The righteous Joseph's dreams that elicited the envy of his brothers,
     Genesis 37:5–11.
21. Charles Dickens, *A Christmas Carol* (Clayton, DE: Prestwick House, Inc.,
     2005).
22. Homer, *The Iliad*, trans. Robert Fagles (New York: Viking Penguin,
     1990), Book 2: 1–47, 99–100.
23. Mortimer Adler, *The Great Ideas: A Syntopicon of the Great Books of the
     Western World*, vol. 2 (Chicago: Encyclopedia Britannica, 1952), 139–140.
24. Joseph Frank, *Dostoevsky: A Writer in His Time* (Princeton, NJ: Princeton
     University Press, 2010), 759.

Chapter 1: The Nous in Hellenic Philosophy: Anaxagoras to Plato

25. Sullivan, "Nous in the Tragedies," 61.
26. Homer, *The Iliad*, 13.730.
27. Bruno Snell, *The Discovery of the Mind in Greek Philosophy and Literature*
     (Mineola, NY: Courier Dover Publications, 1960), 13.
28. Sullivan, "Nous in the Tragedies," 62.
29. *Routledge Encyclopedia of Philosophy*, s.v. "nous."
30. Ibid.

31. Ibid.
32. Ibid., 70.
33. Ibid.
34. Ibid.
35. Copleston, *A History of Philosophy*, 79.
36. *Routledge Encyclopedia of Philosophy*, s.v. "nous."
37. Plato, *Timaeus*, 28a6, cited in *Stanford Encyclopedia of Philosophy*, accessed August 10, 2014, http://plato.stanford.edu/entries/plato-timaeus/.
38. Ibid.
39. Plato, *Phaedrus*, 246a, 253d–254b.
40. Copleston, *A History of Philosophy*, 208.
41. Ibid., 210.
42. Plato, *Republic* Book 6, The University of Adelaide Library, Electronic Texts Collection, accessed July 14, 2014, http://www.faculty.umb.edu/gary_zabel/Courses/Phil%20281b/Philosophy%20of%20Magic/Phil%20100/Readings/Plato%27s%20Republic.htm.
43. Psychology, Philosophy, and Plato's Divided Line, accessed July 25, 2018, http://www.john-uebersax.com/plato/plato1.htm.
44. Plato, *Republic* 515c–517a.
45. Sherrard, *The Rape of Man and Nature*, 17. In discussing Plato's great chain of being, Sherrard uses the Greek term *perichoresis*—a word that expresses the dynamic co-penetration of the uncreated and created, the divine and the human.
46. Ibid., 17–18.

Chapter 2: The *Nous* in Hellenic Philosophy: Aristotle to Plotinus

47. Aristotle, *Metaphysics* xii.7.1072a21-23, cited in Metaphysics, trans. Richard Hope (Ann Arbor, MI: University of Michigan Press, 2007), 258.
48. Accessed August 5, 2018, https://classicalwisdom.com/unmoved-mover/
49. David Bradshaw describes this as follows: "The Prime Mover is the activity of self-thinking thought, it is also actuality in the fullest sense, as both the cause of being for all things and as an existent altogether free of potency, and therefore fully and completely real." *Aristotle East and West*, 44.
50. Aristotle, *De Anima* iii 4, 429a9-10, cited in *Stanford Encyclopedia of Philosophy*. Chapter 7, Mind, accessed August 6, 2018, https://plato.stanford.edu/entries/aristotle-psychology/#4
51. *Webster's Third New International Dictionary*, s.v. "nous."
52. J. L. Ackrill, *Aristotle the Philosopher* (New York: Oxford University Press, 1990), 133.
53. Ibid., 63.

54. Herbert Davidson, *Alfarabi, Avicenna, and Averroes, on Intellect* (Oxford, England: Oxford University Press, 1992), 3.
55. Ackrill, *Aristotle the Philosopher*, 107–109.
56. Aristotle, *Nicomachean Ethics* X.7.1177b26, quoted in Ackrill, *Aristotle the Philosopher*, 138–139.
57. Philip Sherrard, *The Rape of Man and Nature* (Limni, Evia, Greece: Denise Harvey, Publisher, 1991), 46.
58. Accessed August 3, 2018, https://www.britannica.com/story/plato-and-aristotle-how-do-they-differ
59. Sherrard, *The Rape of Man and Nature*, 49.
60. Ibid.
61. Copleston, *A History of Philosophy*, 457.
62. Ibid., 458.
63. Ibid., 460.
64. Ibid., 451.
65. B. N. Tatakis, *Christian Philosophy in the Patristic and Byzantine Tradition* (Rollinsford, NH: Orthodox Research Institute, 2007), 27.
66. Copleston, *A History of Philosophy*, 461.
67. Ibid., 462–463.
68. Ibid., 464.
69. Ibid., 467.
70. The four cardinal virtues are (1) *phronêsis* (prudence/practical wisdom), (2) *dikaiosunê* (justice/morality), (3) *sôphrosunê* (temperance/moderation), (4) *andreia* (fortitude/courage).
71. Copleston, *A History of Philosophy*, 470–472.
72. *Routledge Encyclopedia of Philosophy*, s.v. "nous."
73. Copleston, *A History of Philosophy*, 472.
74. Plotinus, *First Ennead, Great Books of the Western World*, vol. 17, ed. Adler and Hutchins (Chicago: Encyclopedia Britannica, 1952), 25.
75. Ibid.

Chapter 3: A Transition from Hellenic Philosophy to Christianity

76. Dee Pennock, *Path to Sanity: Lessons from Ancient Holy Counselors on How to Have a Sound Mind* (Minneapolis, MN: Light and Life Publishing Company, 2010), 210.
77. James E. Kiefer, "Biographical Sketches of Memorable Christians of the Past," *Justin Martyr: Philosopher, Apologist and Martyr*, accessed June 10, 2014, http://justus.anglican.org/resources/bio/175.html
78. Philip of Side, born in Pamphylia, was a clergyman of St John Chrysostom. Quote taken from: https://archive.org/stream/TheFragmentsOfPhilipOfSideTranslatedIntoEnglish/Philip_of_Side_Fragments_djvu.txt, fragment 2, p. 17, accessed July 12, 2017

79. St Clement of Alexandria, *The Stromata*, Rev. Alexander Roberts and James Donaldson, ed., *The Ante-Nicene Fathers*, vol. 2 (Grand Rapids, MI: Wm. B. Eerdmans Publishing Company, 1956), 323.

80. Pennock, *Path to Sanity*, 217.

81. Richard Gamble, ed., *The Great Tradition* (Wilmington, DE: ISI Books, 2007), 185.

82. Vladimir Lossky, *The Mystical Theology of the Eastern Church* (Cambridge: James Clarke & C., 2005), 49.

83. This term refers back to the higher, Intelligible Realm that appeared in Plato's chart, illustrating the Analogy of the Divided Line on page 6.

84. From an Orthodox Liturgical text of the Troparion of the Royal Hours of Nativity: the full phrase in this translation reads "Christ is born to raise the image that fell of old," accessed July 3, 2018, http://sergei.synology.me/text/readings-variables/RoyalHours_Nativity_2018.pdf.

85. Tatakis, *Christian Philosophy in the Patristic and Byzantine Tradition*, 22.

Chapter 4: The Incarnation and Deification in Early Patristic Thought

86. St John of Damascus, *An Exact Exposition of the Orthodox Faith*.

87. St Irenaeus, *Against Heresies, The Ante-Nicene Fathers*, vol. 1 (Grand Rapids, MI: WM. B. Eerdmans Publishing Co., 1987), Book V, Preface, 526.

88. St Athanasius of Alexandria, *On the Incarnation*, 54:3, 107. The actual wording in this source is as follows: "For he was incarnate that we might be made god."

89. St Symeon the New Theologian, *The First Created Man*, Homily 45:3, trans. Father Seraphim Rose (Platina, CA: St. Herman of Alaska Brotherhood, 2013), 96–97.

90. A compilation of these patristic quotes is available in Michael Paul Gama, *Theosis* (Eugene, Oregon: Wipf & Stock, 2017), 103.

91. Sherrard, *The Rape of Man and Nature*, 21.

92. Ibid., 12–13.

93. Ibid., 28–29.

94. Ibid.

95. St Maximus the Confessor, *On the Cosmic Mystery of Jesus Christ, Ad Thalassium 60*, Crestwood, NJ: St. Vladimir's Press, 2003, 126.

96. Timothy Ware, *The Orthodox Church* (Harmondsworth, Middlesex, England: Penguin Books, 1964), 77.

97. Ibid., 78.

98. David Bradshaw, "The Divine Energies in the New Testament," *St. Vladimir's Theological Quarterly* 50, no. 3 (2006): 189. For a comprehensive explanation of *energeia*, see also Bradshaw's *Aristotle East and West*.

Chapter 5: The Heart and the *Nous* in Patristic Thought

99. Bradshaw, *Aristotle East and West*, 196.
100. Ibid.
101. Ware, *The Orthodox Church*, 74. The author is referring to the teaching of St Macarius of Egypt, AD 300.
102 Pseudo Macarius, *Fifty Homilies and the Great Letter*, 43.7, trans. Maloney (New York: Paulist Press, 1992), as quoted in Bradshaw, *Aristotle East and West*, 197.
103. St Gregory Palamas, *The Triads*, C I. ii. 3, 43.
104. David Bradshaw, "The Mind and the Heart in the Christian East and West," *Faith and Philosophy* 26, no. 5 (2009): 582.
105. Ibid., 581.
106. Ibid., 582.
107. Ibid.

Chapter 6: Purification of the *Nous*

108. St Symeon the New Theologian, *The First-Created Man*, Homily 37.4, trans. Father Seraphim Rose (Platina, CA: St. Herman of Alaska Brotherhood, 2013), 71.
109. Lossky, *The Mystical Theology of the Eastern Church*, 17.
110. The prayer most often employed in hesychastic practice is the Jesus prayer: *Lord Jesus Christ, Son of God, have mercy on me a sinner*, similar to the words mentioned in Christ's parable of the publican and Pharisee (Luke 18:13). Through practice of this prayer and the guarding of the *nous* from extraneous thoughts, the hesychasts were able to draw closer to God. A humble, repentant heart and the constant remembrance of God are essential for the effectiveness of this prayer. See Ware, *The Orthodox Church*, 74–75. The Holy Fathers discourage the use of the prayer of the heart or the "Jesus prayer" without the guidance of an experienced pastor or elder.
111. St Gregory Palamas, *The Triads*, B I. iii. 4, 32.
112. Hierotheos, *Orthodox Psychotherapy*, 128.
113. Ibid., 139. St Thalassios the Libyan was a contemporary of St Maximus the Confessor.
114. Hierotheos, *Orthodox Psychotherapy*, 128.
115. Ibid., 135.
116. Ibid., 136.
117. St Theophan the Recluse, *Thoughts for Each Day of the Year* (Thursday of the Second Week of Lent), trans. Lisa Marie Baranov (Platina, CA: St. Herman of Alaska Brotherhood, 2012), 60–61.
118. St Basil the Great, Letter 2 to St Gregory Nazianzus, as quoted by Metropolitan Hierotheos in *St. Gregory Palamas as a Hagiorite*, 386.

119. Bradshaw, "The Mind and Heart," 597.
120. Hierotheos, *Orthodox Psychotherapy*, 254–255.

Chapter 7: A Move Away from Noetic Perception

121. Sherrard, *The Rape of Man and Nature*, 28–29.
122. Ibid., 14–15.
123. For a more detailed explanation of Augustine's doctrine of divine simplicity, see Bradshaw, *Aristotle East and West*, 224.
124. Father Seraphim Rose, *The Place of Blessed Augustine in the Orthodox Church* (Platina, CA: St. Herman of Alaska Brotherhood, 1996), 36.
125. Ibid.
126. Ibid., 40.
127. Philip Sherrard, *The Greek East and Latin West* (Limni, Evia, Greece: Denise Harvey, Publisher, 1959), 143.
128. Although *intellectus* is the correct Latin translation of the Greek *nous*, it retains the meaning found in the philosophical works of Aristotle, rather than the Eastern patristic interpretation.
129. Ibid.
130. Ibid., 156.
131. The term *nous* in Greek was indeed translated as *intellectus* into Latin, but the source was the philosophical works of Aristotle, not the Greek patristic texts of the Eastern Church.
132. Ibid., 158.
133. Thomas Aquinas, *Summa of the Summa*, ed. Peter Kreeft (San Francisco: Ignatius Press, 1990), 16.
134. Peter Kreeft, Introduction to *Summa of the Summa*, xiii.
135. Ralph McInerny, *St. Thomas Aquinas* (Boston, MA: G.K. Hall & Co., 1977), 80.
136. Aquinas, *Summa of the Summa*, [I, 79, 9], 279.
137. Sherrard, *The Rape of Man and Nature*, 50–51.
138. Thomas Aquinas, *Contra Errores Graecorum*, trans. Peter Damian Fehlman, accessed June 10, 2014, http://dhspriory.org/thomas/ContraErrGraecorum.htm.
139. Sherrard, *The Greek East and Latin West*, 153.
140. Ibid., 153–154.
141. St Gregory Palamas, *The Triads*, Introduction, 1.
142. Hierotheos, *Saint Gregory Palamas as a Hagiorite*, 25.
143. St Gregory Palamas, *The Triads*, Introduction, 21.
144. Mortimer J. Adler, *Introduction and Syntopical Guide*, Gateway to the Great Books, Chapter 5, Philosophy (Chicago, Illinois: Encyclopedia Britannica, Inc. William Benton, Publisher, 1963), 94.

Chapter 8: Biographical Details

145. Frank, *Dostoevsky: A Writer in His Time*, 23.
146. Ibid., 24.
147. Ibid., 30.
148. Ibid., 24.
149. Ibid., 25.
150. Ibid.
151. Ibid., 56–57.
152. Ibid., 34.
153. Ibid., 35.
154. Literature Resource Center, *Fyodor M. Dostoevsky*, accessed July 14, 2014, http://people.brandeis.edu/~teuber/dostoevskybio .html#BiographicalInfoEssay.
155. Konstantin Mochulsky, *Dostoevsky, His Life and Work*, trans. Michael A. Minihan (Princeton, NJ: Princeton University Press, 1971), 147.
156. Christian Classics Ethereal Library, *Fyodor Dostoevsky, Russian Novelist*, accessed September 28, 2014, http://www.ccel.org/ccel/dostoevsky.
157. Frank, *Dostoevsky*, Preface, xv–xvi.
158. Ibid., 89.
159. Mochulsky, *Dostoevsky, His Life and Work*, Chronology, xxix. Dostoevsky first married a widow, Maria Isayeva, who had a son from a previous marriage.
160. http://people.brandeis.edu/~teuber/dostoevskybio.html#Biographical InfoEssay.
161. Frank, *Dostoevsky*, 769.
162. Anna Dostoevsky, *Dostoevsky: Reminiscences*, trans. Beatrice Stillman (New York: Liveright Publishing Corp., 1971), 305.
163. Ibid., 92.

Chapter 9: "The Dream of a Ridiculous Man": Synopsis and Analysis of the Story

164. Fyodor Dostoevsky, "The Dream of a Ridiculous Man," in *The Best Short Stories of Fyodor Dostoevsky*, trans. David Magarshack (New York: The Modern Library, 2001), 263.
165. Ibid., 264.
166. Ibid., 271.
167. Nun Ioanna Pomazansky, "What Is the Heart?" *Orthodox Life* 62, no. 6 (November–December 2011): 33.
168. Ibid., 24.
169. St Macarius the Egyptian, *Fifty Spiritual Homilies*, quoted in Hierotheos' *Orthodox Psychotherapy*, 164. Also at http://archive.org/stream/ fiftyspiritualhooopseuuoft/fiftyspiritualhooopseuuoft_djvu.txt, accessed September 12, 2014.

170. Archbishop Luke Voyno-Yasenetsky, *Дух, душа и тело* [*Spirit, Soul and Body*], ed. N. G. Kutsayeva (Minsk: Byelorussian Publishing House, 2013), 102. Biographical note: Archbishop Luke Voyno-Yasenetsky of Simferopol (1877–1961) was a famous medical researcher and surgeon in the Soviet Union. He continued his surgical practice even after becoming an archbishop. For his staunch confession of the Christian faith under the atheistic regime, he was canonized by the Patriarchate of Russia in 1996. By making the statement "self-awareness is a function of the spirit, not the mind," Archbishop Luke supports the thought of St Macarius the Great and other Church fathers as to the actual physical location of the spirit within the heart and not the brain.
171. Dostoevsky, "Dream of a Ridiculous Man," 272.
172. Ibid.
173. Ibid., 273.
174. Ibid.
175. Ibid.
176. Ibid.
177. Ibid.
178. Ibid.
179. Ibid., 275.
180. Ibid.
181. Ibid.
182. Ibid.
183. Ibid., 275–276.
184. Ibid., 276.
185. Ibid., 279.
186. Ibid.
187. Ibid., 280.
188. Saint Gregory Palamas, *The Triads*, E III i. 29, 84.
189. Dostoevsky, "Dream of a Ridiculous Man," 280.
190. Frank, *Dostoevsky*, 758.
191. Jordan B. Peterson, *12 Rules for Life; An Antidote to Chaos* (Toronto: Random House Canada, 2018), 176.
192. Ibid., 50.
193. Ibid., 54.
194. Dostoevsky, "Dream of a Ridiculous Man," 281.
195. Ibid.
196. Ibid.
197. Sherrard, *The Rape of Man and Nature*, 25.
198. Dostoevsky, "Dream of a Ridiculous Man," 281–282.
199. St Augustine of Hippo, *City of God, Nicene and Post Nicene Fathers*, vol. 2, ed. Philip Schaff (Peabody, MA: Hendrickson Publishers, 1995), 282–283.

200. Dostoevsky, "Dream of a Ridiculous Man," 282.
201. Ibid., 283.
202. Ibid.
203. Ibid., 285.
204. Ibid.
205. Ibid.
206. Ivan Ilyin, Аксиомы религиозного опыта [Axioms of Religious Experience], 303 (Translated and abbreviated from the Russian—MN).
207. Mochulsky, *Dostoevsky, His Life and Work*, 577.
208. Hierotheos, *Orthodox Psychotherapy*, 109.

Chapter 10: Examples of Other "Ridiculous Men" in Dostoevsky's Novels

209. David Magarshack, trans., from the Introduction to *The Best Short Stories of Fyodor Dostoevsky*, ix.
210. Ibid., Introduction, xx.
211. Justin Popovich (1894–1979), a prominent theologian and Dostoevsky scholar, canonized by the Serbian Orthodox Church in 2010.
212. Archimandrite Justin Popovich, *Философия и религия Ф. М. Достоевского* [*The Philosophy and Religion of F. M. Dostoevsky*], a translation from Serbian into Russian (Minsk: D. V. Harchenko, 2008), 8–9.
213. Fyodor Dostoevsky, *The Idiot*, trans. Richard Pevear and Larissa Volokhonsky (New York: Vintage Books, A Division of Random House, 2001), 6.
214. Ibid., 225–226.
215. Ibid., 6–7.
216. Ibid., 54.
217. Ibid., 139.
218. Ibid., Introduction, xii.
219. Ibid.
220. Ibid., Introduction, xiv.
221. Ibid., Introduction, xvi.
222. Ibid., xix.
223. Sherrard, *The Rape of Man and Nature*, 25.
224. Fyodor Dostoevsky, *The Brothers Karamazov*, trans. Richard Pevear and Larissa Volokhonsky (New York: Farrar, Straus and Giroux, 1990), 18.
225. Ibid., 330.
226. Funerals in the Orthodox Church take place on the third day after the repose. In the days prior to the burial service, the Psalter is read over a deceased layperson and the Gospel if the reposed was a priest.
227. Dostoevsky, *The Brothers Karamazov*, 362.
228. Ibid., 362–363.

229. Dostoevsky, "Dream of a Ridiculous Man," 275.
230. Hierotheos, *St. Gregory Palamas as a Hagiorite*, 243.
231. Dostoevsky, "Dream of a Ridiculous Man," 285.
232. Dostoevsky, *The Brothers Karamazov*, 287.
233. Ibid., 288.
234. Ibid.
235. Ibid., 289.
236. Ibid.
237. Fyodor Dostoevsky, *Demons*, trans. Richard Pevear and Larissa Volokhonsky (New York: Vintage Books, A Division of Random House, 1995), 43.
238. Ibid., 44.
239. Dostoevsky, *Demons*, 47.
240. This chapter was dropped from the first printing because of censorship (see Introduction, xxvi) and is included in this edition in an Appendix. I believe that without it, the character of Nikolai Stavrogin is not fully revealed.
241. Dostoevsky, *Demons*, 692–693.
242. Ibid., 707.
243. Ibid., 707–708.
244. Ibid., 709.

Chapter 11: References to the Unnamed *Nous*

245. deiform: God-like in form or character.
246. Josef Pieper, *Leisure: The Basis of Culture* (San Francisco: Ignatius Press, 2009), 28–29.
247. Martin Heidegger, *Introduction to Metaphysics*, trans. Gregory Fried and Richard Polt (New Haven, CT: Yale University Press, 2000), 60.
248. Ibid., 14.
249. Ibid., 112.
250. Ibid., 102–103.
251. Ibid., 206.
252. Ibid., 14.
253. Ibid., 207.
254. Ibid., 199.
255. Ibid., 201.
256. William F. Lynch, *Christ and Apollo: The Dimensions of the Literary Imagination* (Wilmington, DE: ISI Books, 2003), 158–159.
257. Ibid., 11.
258. Ibid., 31.
259. Ibid., 33.
260. Ibid., 35.

261. Ibid., 37.
262. C. S. Lewis, *Mere Christianity* (San Francisco: HarperCollins Publishers, 1980), 220.
263. Ibid., 221.
264. Chris Jensen, "Shine as the Sun: C. S. Lewis and the Doctrine of Deification," *In Pursuit of Truth: A Journal of Christian Scholarship*, October 2007, accessed October 1, 2014, http://www.cslewis.org/journal/shine-as-the-sun-cs-lewis-and-the-doctrine-of-deification/

Chapter 12: A Renewed Interest in Deification

265. "Catechism of the Catholic Church 1: 2: 2: 3: 1: 1: 459–460," *The Holy See*, n.d., accessed August 22, 2014.
266. Pope John Paul II, "Orientale Lumen," *The Holy See*, May 2, 1995, accessed August 22, 2014.
267. Gama, *Theosis*, 9.
268. Ibid., 10.
269. See Part I, Chapter 4.
270. Gama, *Theosis*, 126.
271. Ilyin, *Axioms of Religious Experience*, 95.

Chapter 13: Contemporary Orthodox Writers on the Nous

272. Frederica Mathewes-Green, *Welcome to the Orthodox Church: An Introduction to Eastern Christianity* (Brewster, MA: Paraclete Press, 2015), 196.
273. Ibid., 198–199.
274. Ibid., 200–201.
275. Ibid., 202.
276. Albert S. Rossi, *Becoming a Healing Presence* (Chesterton, IN: Ancient Faith Publishing, 2014), 22.
277. Ibid., 55–56.
278. Abbot Nikon Vorobiev, *Letters to Spiritual Children* (Richfield Springs, NY: Nikodemos Orthodox Publication Society, 2015), 11.

Conclusion

279. St Anthony (251–356 AD) lived in strict asceticism in the Egyptian desert.
280. Bishop Nikolai Velimirovich, *Missionary Letters*, trans. Hieromonk Serafim Baltic, Part 3: Letters 201–300 (Grayslake, IL: Joe Buley Memorial Library/New Gracanica Monastery, 2011), Letter 243 (page 383 in Russian translation).
281. Ivan Ilyin, *Axioms of Religious Experience*, Chapter 1, "On the Subjectivity of Religious Experience," trans. G. E. Henderson (M. Div paper, South Canaan, PA: St. Tikhon's Theological Seminary, 2009), 10.

INDEX